TRUE CRIME CASE HISTORIES - VOLUME 17

12 DISTURBING TRUE CRIME STORIES

JASON NEAL

Cover images of:

Brian Wells (top-left)

John Calvaresi: (top-right)

Michael Boettlin: (bottom-left)

Katherine Knight: (bottom-right)

More books by Jason Neal

Looking for more?? I am constantly adding new volumes of True Crime Case Histories. The series **can be read in any order**, and all books are available in paperback, hardcover, and audiobook.

Check out the complete series at:

https://amazon.com/author/jason-neal

All Jason Neal books are also available in **AudioBook format at Audible.com.** Enjoy a **Free Audiobook** when you signup for a 30-Day trial using this link:

https://geni.us/AudibleTrueCrime

FREE BONUS EBOOK FOR MY READERS

As my way of saying "Thank you" for downloading, I'm giving away a FREE True Crime e-book I think you'll enjoy.

https://TrueCrimeCaseHistories.com

Just visit the link above to let me know where to send your free book!

CONTENTS

INTRODUCTION

If you've read the previous volumes of *True Crime Case Histories*, you already know what to expect—stories of real crimes, carefully reconstructed and presented without censorship or sensationalism.

If this is your first time, consider this a brief warning: These aren't dramatizations or sanitized summaries. These stories can be graphic and disturbing. Oftentimes, true crime television shows or news stories can gloss over the gruesome parts, but in my books, I do my best to give you every detail, regardless of how unsettling they may be.

I include these details not to sensationalize, but to provide readers with a deeper understanding of the killer's mind. Although it might be impossible for us to grasp their motives fully, the sheer magnitude of their depravity will keep you turning pages.

Each story in this book has been meticulously researched using court transcripts, police files, autopsy reports, and first-hand testimony. Many are little-known cases, long forgotten by the media but remembered all too vividly by the people they affected.

Many of the stories in this volume were suggested by readers who remembered them from their own hometowns or were personally affected by the events. Some are recent, others decades old, but all are shocking.

Each of these cases reveals something different: calculated cruelty, unchecked obsession, shattered families, and the staggering depths of human depravity. Some were solved by luck, others by science. A few almost got away.

For case photos, court records, and bonus materials related to this volume, please visit:

TrueCrimeCaseHistories.com/vol17

To join my mailing list for updates and a free e-book, visit:

TrueCrimeCaseHistories.com

Thanks for reading,

Jason Neal

CHAPTER 1
THE BUTCHER OF ABERDEEN

Aberdeen is a quaint coal mining town nestled in the fertile Hunter Valley of New South Wales, Australia. With a population of just under 2,000 people, it's the kind of place where everyone knows everyone else's business. This sleepy community sits about 180 miles north of Sydney among rolling hills and pastures dotted with cattle and sheep. Historic buildings dating back to the 1800s line its main street, giving it a charming old-world feel that masks the horror that would unfold there one fateful night.

Most residents work in the nearby coal mines or on surrounding farms. Life moves at a steady pace in Aberdeen —people wave to each other on the street, gather at the local pub after work, and generally keep to themselves. It's not the sort of place where you'd expect to find yourself at the center of national headlines.

That all changed on a late February night in 2000, when this peaceful town became the setting for one of the most disturbing crimes in Australian history—a horror so gruesome that it would make hardened police officers vomit at the scene.

In the late afternoon of February 29, John Price finished his shift at the local mines where he'd worked for seventeen years. The forty-five-year-old father of three had warned his coworkers earlier that same day, "If I'm not here tomorrow, it's because Kath killed me." Those ominous words would come to haunt everyone who knew him.

Just hours earlier, Price had appeared before a magistrate to take out a restraining order against his partner, Katherine Knight. The pair had been in a volatile relationship for five years, and Price had finally reached his breaking point. Katherine Knight had stabbed him in the chest during an argument a few days before, and although the wound wasn't severe, it served as a clear-cut warning—one that, unfortunately, came too late.

That night, Price stopped at a neighbor's house before heading home. During the visit, he seemed agitated but attempted to conceal it through casual conversation. As night came, he said goodnight to his friends. He walked home the short distance to his simple one-story house, not knowing it was his last night on Earth.

Meanwhile, Katherine Knight was on a path toward something unspeakable—an eruption of violence that would soon horrify the entire nation.

Katherine Mary Knight was born in October 1955 to a dysfunctional family in the small town of Tenterfield, about 270 miles north of Sydney. Her early life was marred by violence and instability. She claimed she had been sexually abused by several male relatives throughout her childhood, though her claims were never verified. Meanwhile, former classmates remembered her as a bully who exhibited aggressive behavior from an early age.

Katherine's adulthood followed the turbulent pattern of her childhood. At nineteen, she married David Kellett in 1974. This marriage set the tone for her future relationships. On their wedding night, an inebriated Kellett fell asleep after sex, and Katherine, in a rage at feeling ignored, tried to strangle him. This incident was a precursor to the violence to come.

Katherine's explosive outbursts punctuated their marriage. In one incident, while she was in the later stages of her pregnancy, she struck Kellett in the back of the head with a frying pan as he returned home after a darts competition. Kellett sought medical treatment for a fractured skull, but Katherine convinced him to drop the charges.

After their first child was born in 1976, Kellett left Katherine for another woman. Katherine's reaction was extreme: She kidnapped their infant daughter and placed the baby on railroad tracks before threatening a woman at knifepoint and taking a young boy hostage. Police subdued her and transported her to a psychiatric hospital. However, she was released shortly after. Remarkably, Kellett was so frightened by Katherine's actions that he returned to Aberdeen to support her. The couple had another daughter in 1980, but by 1984, Katherine had left Kellett for good.

Katherine's later relationships followed the same violent pattern. In the late 1980s, she lived with David Saunders, a local miner. Her jealousy manifested in horrifying ways. She wanted to teach Saunders a lesson about cheating, so she cut the throat of his two-month-old dingo puppy right in front of him. Then she knocked him unconscious with a frying pan. Despite this traumatic episode, they remained together and had a child in 1988. However, after Katherine attacked Saunders with an iron and stabbed him with scissors, he fled into hiding. Katherine then filed a police report claiming she was the victim of abuse and obtained a restraining order against Saunders.

After that relationship fell apart, Knight then took up with John Chillingworth, with whom she had a son in 1992. A few years later, she left Chillingworth for John Price.

Throughout these tumultuous years, Katherine built a career as a slaughterhouse worker at the local meat processing plant. She excelled in the environment and was known for her skill with knives and cleavers. She took pride in her work, decorating the walls of her home with animal skins, skulls, and butchering tools—a macabre foreshadowing of the horror to come.

By all accounts, Katherine Knight was a walking contradiction. She could be charming and hardworking, but she could also explode into violent rages at the slightest provocation. Psychiatric evaluations later revealed she suffered from borderline personality disorder, a condition often linked to childhood trauma and characterized by unstable relationships and impulsive aggression. However, experts emphasized that this condition did not render her incapable of distinguishing right from wrong.

John Price came into Katherine Knight's life around 1995. Born the same year as Knight, Price was well-liked in Aberdeen, described by friends as a "terrific bloke" who was generous and outgoing. After divorcing in 1988, he lived with two of his three children in the home where he would ultimately meet his tragic end.

When John and Katherine began dating, the locals expressed concern. Price knew about Knight's violent reputation but believed his love would change her. Price often described the early days of their relationship as "a bunch of roses," and his children reportedly liked Katherine. To outsiders, they appeared to be a normal couple despite the occasional argument.

Over time, however, the relationship deteriorated. In 1998, Katherine wanted to get married, but John refused. In retaliation, she sent a video to Price's employer showing items she claimed he had stolen from work—outdated medical kits he had scavenged from company trash. Despite their minimal value, Price was fired from his job of seventeen years. Furious at this betrayal, Price kicked Knight out of his house and ended the relationship.

Astonishingly, they eventually reconciled, but on Price's terms. He allowed Knight to spend time with him but refused to let her move back into his home or share his finances. This arrangement only increased Knight's insecurity and resentment, and their fighting intensified. Many of Price's friends avoided him whenever Knight was around, unwilling to tolerate the drama she brought.

By February 2000, their relationship had reached a breaking point. Katherine's erratic behavior had escalated, culminating in her stabbing Price in the chest during an argument. Though the wound wasn't fatal, it was the wake-up call Price needed. On February 28, 2000, he went to court and obtained a restraining order against Knight. That same day, he confided to coworkers that he feared for his life, even telling one colleague that if he didn't show up for work the next day, it would mean Knight had killed him.

Price went home that night, even with the restraining order and his fears; he worried that Katherine might hurt his kids if he stayed away. It was a decision that would cost him his life.

On the evening of February 29, 2000, John Price behaved as usual after work, spending time with neighbors before returning home around 11:00 p.m. Unknown to Price, Knight had already arranged for his two older children to stay at a friend's house that night, ensuring he would be alone. When Price arrived home, Knight wasn't there, and he went to bed just after 11:00 p.m.

Meanwhile, Knight was preparing for her final, gruesome confrontation. That afternoon, she had purchased a new black lingerie outfit and made strange comments to her children while videotaping them, almost as if recording a farewell message. She arrived at Price's house later that night while he was asleep. With chilling composure, she let herself in, watched television briefly, and took a shower before waking Price.

Wearing the black negligee, Knight initiated sex with Price, and he obliged. For a fleeting moment, the horrific events to follow were delayed by a façade of intimacy. Price then fell asleep, unaware that his partner was merely lulling him into a false sense of security.

In the early hours of March 1, 2000, Katherine Knight retrieved a large butcher's knife and attacked John Price as he slept. The first thrust pierced his chest, jolting him awake into a living nightmare. Blood evidence later showed that Price made a frantic attempt to escape. Injured and bleeding, he staggered out of his bedroom and down the hall, trying to reach either the front door or a light switch.

Knight pursued him through the house as he struggled to escape. Price made it to the front door and got outside, leaving a trail of blood in the doorway. However, he either collapsed from blood loss on the porch, or Knight dragged him back inside. He fell in the hallway just inside the house, where he bled to death from his numerous injuries. An autopsy would later reveal at least thirty-seven stab wounds to his front and back, with damage to several vital organs.

But Katherine Knight's night of horror had only begun. In the aftermath of the killing, she exhibited a level of calm, calculated butchery that defies comprehension. According to the investigation, Knight left the house shortly after the murder and drove into town to withdraw $1,000 from Price's bank account via ATM. She then returned to the blood-soaked home and set about mutilating Price's body with the expertise her career had afforded her.

Katherine Knight

Using her razor-sharp knives and years of meat-working experience, Katherine Knight skinned Price's entire corpse. She removed his skin in one piece with remarkable skill and a steady hand, achieving one full pelt that included the skin of his face, ears, nose, torso, genitals, and limbs. She then hung this skin on a meat hook affixed to the top frame of the lounge room door. The forensic pathologist later found that the skin was so intact that it could be re-sewn onto Price's body during the autopsy, demonstrating the precision of Knight's flaying work.

Knight then decapitated Price, cutting off his head and carrying it into the kitchen, before she proceeded to cook some of his body parts. She placed his decapitated head in a large pot on the stove, added vegetables—potatoes, pumpkin, cabbage, zucchini, squash, and beetroot—and boiled them together to create a macabre stew.

She also sliced off strips of flesh from Price's buttocks and baked them in the oven with more vegetables. Once these "roasts" were done, Knight arranged the cooked meat and vegetables on dinner plates as if serving a meal. She set two place settings at the dining table, complete with notes beside each plate bearing the names of Price's children. Knight intended to serve this horrific cannibal feast to Price's son and daughter—a final act of perverse brutality.

Knight then took Price's head out of the pot and placed it in a serving dish. She arranged what remained of his decapitated, skinless body on the living room floor. In a final bizarre gesture of contempt, Knight posed the body by crossing Price's legs and draping his left arm over an empty soda bottle as if in a casual lounging position.

Near the body, Knight left a handwritten note atop a photograph of Price, serving as a twisted justification for her actions. Scrawled with blood and bits of flesh, the note accused Price of terrible crimes, including raping her daughter and abusing his own children. The accusations were entirely groundless, as investigators would later confirm.

Having staged this grotesque scene, Knight attempted to take her own life—or at least render herself unconscious by swallowing a large number of pills. She later claimed this was a suicide attempt, but the amount she took was not lethal. It caused her to lose consciousness and slip into a comatose state on the floor of the home, which was how the police would find her when they arrived.

At 6:00 a.m. on March 1, 2000, neighbors noticed something was amiss at John Price's house. His work truck was in the driveway, which was unusual because he usually left early for his job. Concerned coworkers, remembering Price's ominous warning, sent a colleague to check on him when he didn't show up for work. That colleague and a worried neighbor met at the house. They knocked on the bedroom window and called out, but there was no response. Through a doorway, they spotted what looked like blood smears on the front door and immediately contacted the police.

Local Aberdeen police arrived at the scene shortly after receiving the call. Two officers approached the front door, where they saw blood on the door frame. Receiving no answer, they forced entry into the house and encountered a scene so ghastly that many of the responding officers would later need counseling.

In the entryway and hall, they discovered Price's headless, skinned body lying on the floor, grotesquely draped over a bottle. His skin was hanging nearby. On the kitchen table, police found two place settings with meals prepared—plates of cooked meat and vegetables, each labeled with a note bearing Price's children's names. The food was still warm, with a pot on the stove gently simmering with the horrific stew.

Amid this carnage, officers found Katherine Knight unconscious on the floor in a bedroom, having overdosed on pills. Knight showed no immediate reaction as the officers secured the scene. They had to carry her out on a stretcher, given her comatose state, and an ambulance rushed her to the hospital for treatment.

With Knight in custody, investigators began the grim task of processing the crime scene. They took photographs, many of which authorities deemed so graphic that they sealed them from public access. Forensic examiners documented the extensive blood trails throughout the house, showing the path of Price's futile escape attempt and the struggle. A butcher's knife, one of Knight's own from her work kit, lay coated with Price's blood near the bed.

The autopsy confirmed the ferocity of the attack: at least thirty-seven stab wounds, deep and penetrating, including injuries to vital organs such as the lungs, liver, and aorta. Many wounds were on the front of the body, but numerous stab injuries were also found on his back, indicating he had been stabbed from behind as he tried to escape. Defensive wounds on Price's hands and arms showed he had tried to ward off the knife. The pathologist also cataloged the post-mortem mutilations: the complete skinning, decapitation, and butchering of the body.

When Katherine Knight awoke from her drugged stupor at the hospital, she initially claimed to have no memory of what had happened the night before. She feigned confusion and amnesia when the police began questioning her. However, the evidence was overwhelming. On March 2, 2000, as soon as she was physically well enough, Katherine Knight was formally charged with the murder of John Price.

The brutality of Katherine Knight's crime posed a challenge to the New South Wales justice system. She was arraigned in March 2001 and, defying the evidence, entered a plea of not guilty. The trial was scheduled for July 2001 but had to be postponed when one of Knight's attorneys fell ill. It was rescheduled for October 15, 2001.

When the trial date arrived, the court took extraordinary precautions in anticipation of the graphic evidence to be presented. The presiding judge addressed the sixty potential jurors and gave them an unprecedented warning: Because of the extremely disturbing photographs and details they would see, anyone could opt out of serving on the jury if they felt unable to handle it. Five people accepted the excuse and were dismissed immediately.

To everyone's surprise, before any testimony was heard, Knight's defense team announced that she would change her plea to guilty. Knight had instructed her attorneys to seek a plea change after hearing the prosecution's opening statement, possibly realizing the futility of contesting the case. The trial was abruptly aborted on its second day.

The judge adjourned proceedings for the day and ordered a psychiatric evaluation to ensure that Knight was mentally fit to make a guilty plea and understood the consequences. Two psychiatrists examined her and found that while Knight did have borderline personality disorder, she was sane and knew right from wrong. They also noted Knight's claims of amnesia regarding the crime, but they did not find these claims credible enough to prevent her plea. Satisfied that the plea was voluntary, the judge reconvened the court. On

October 18, 2001, Katherine Knight's guilty plea to the murder of John Price was formally accepted.

Knight never gave any official reason for her sudden reversal to a guilty plea. Some speculate that the mountain of evidence—and perhaps the prospect of seeing the photographic proof of her deeds displayed in court—prompted her to concede. Still, despite pleading guilty, she refused to fully accept responsibility for the act and continued to claim memory loss about the mutilation and cannibalism.

During the sentencing hearing in November 2001, Knight's lawyers petitioned to have her excused from hearing the gory details of her own crime, presumably to spare her feelings. The judge denied the request. When the pathologist took the stand and methodically described the condition of Price's body, Knight broke down in the dock, sobbing and wailing. She became so hysterical that the court adjourned, and she had to be sedated.

On November 8, 2001, the judge delivered a scathing sentencing judgment. He recounted the viciousness of the attack and the almost unimaginable defilement of Price's body. He noted that Knight had been motivated by spite and vengeance, essentially punishing Price for trying to leave her. The judge emphasized how meticulously and calmly Knight had committed the post-mortem acts, showing cognition, planning, and surgical precision. Far from an uncontrollable frenzy, her actions were calculated, indicating she took a form of satisfaction in them.

Given the extreme and unprecedented nature of the crime, the judge concluded that only the harshest penalty available was appropriate. Knight's history of violence and lack of remorse led him to deem her an ongoing danger to society. He sentenced Katherine Mary Knight to life imprisonment and refused to set any non-parole period, meaning there was to be no possibility of release. Furthermore, he ordered that her prison papers be marked "Never to be Released"—an order never before imposed on a woman in Australia. With that, Katherine Knight became the first Australian woman to receive a true life sentence without parole.

Knight showed little reaction to the sentence. Price's family expressed relief at the outcome, feeling that anything less than life without parole would not have been justice for John.

In 2006, Knight appealed her sentence to the New South Wales Court of Criminal Appeal. She did not contest her conviction, only the penalty. Her lawyers argued that a life sentence without parole was too harsh. They pointed out her plea and personal circumstances, and they also claimed the judge did not fully consider Knight's mental state. They noted her alleged psychotic episode during the crime and her history of trauma and abuse.

The Crown prosecutor argued that the sentencing judge had looked at all key factors. They stated that the sentence matched the crime's severity. In September 2006, the court dismissed Knight's appeal. The chief justice noted, "This was an appalling crime, almost beyond contemplation in a civilized society." The appellate court found no mistakes in the original sentence; they agreed that Knight's actions fell into the most heinous category imaginable.

Katherine Knight was moved to Silverwater Women's Correctional Centre in New South Wales to serve her life sentence. Her inmate file displayed "Never to be Released" in bold letters.

In prison, Knight has reportedly been a relatively compliant prisoner. She has taken on a "mother hen" role among inmates, working as a mentor and mediating minor disputes between other prisoners. By 2017, officials noted that Knight had a clean prison record with no violent incidents within the facility. Now in her late 60s, Katherine Knight will die in custody, having exhausted her appeals and with no possibility of parole.

When details of the killing emerged in the media, news outlets struggled with how to report the extreme gore. Many included warnings due to the graphic content. The tabloids dubbed Katherine Knight "Australia's Hannibal Lecter" and called her a "cannibal killer"—although technically, there was no confirmed act of cannibalism since Knight didn't get to feed anyone the food. Still, the intended cannibalism cemented her infamy.

The police officers who worked the case were profoundly affected. The first officer on the scene knew John Price personally, making the discovery even more traumatic. Police officers who witnessed the scene required counseling and time off to recover from the psychological toll.

The Katherine Knight case prompted considerable analysis from psychologists, criminologists, and law enforcement professionals. It also challenged stereotypes about female offenders, as women rarely commit such savage acts of violence. Furthermore, Knight's borderline personality disorder, while significant, did not explain or excuse her behavior. Experts emphasized that Knight knew exactly what she was doing, noting that her actions demonstrated planning and goal-oriented anger, not psychosis or loss of reality.

Experts largely disregarded Knight's claims of amnesia. While memory can be unreliable during high stress or intoxication, most agreed she was neither in a fugue state nor hallucinating. The court psychiatrist and later commentators saw her "I don't remember it" defense as a convenient way to avoid talking about the gruesome details.

Criminologists have remarked on how rare it is for a female perpetrator to commit this kind of crime. Women commit a small fraction of homicides overall, and when they do, the circumstances are usually very different, often defensive or involving abuse or less violent methods like poison. Knight's case shattered assumptions about female killers.

Those who knew John Price quietly honor his memory. While Knight gained notorious headlines, Price's family sought privacy. At the sentencing, one of Price's relatives submitted a statement saying that John was a kind, loving man and that Knight had taken a father away from his children in an unimaginably cruel manner. Price's children expressed relief at the sentence through police representatives and asked others to remember their father not for how he died but for how he lived—as a hardworking man who loved his kids and helped others.

Many people in Aberdeen avoided the murder house for years. It stayed empty until it was renovated and got a new look. Residents say that, even decades later, the town hasn't forgotten what happened at that house on that leap day in 2000. It remains a grim point of local lore and a source of lingering sadness.

CHAPTER 2
THE HOUSE ON LANGWORTHY ROAD

The winter of 1992 in Manchester, England, was particularly cold. A bitter chill had settled over the industrial city's east side, where rows of modest houses lined narrow streets in the working-class neighborhood of Moston. The Christmas lights that decorated some of the homes created a cheerful veneer, but behind the doors of 97 Langworthy Road, a horror was unfolding that would shock even the most seasoned detectives.

On December 14, 1992, two men driving along a remote country lane near Werneth Low, about thirteen miles southeast of Manchester, noticed what appeared to be a badly injured person stumbling toward the road. As they approached, they were confronted with a sight that would haunt them for the rest of their lives.

A teenage girl—her body charred black, her skin peeling away in patches, and her hair completely burned off—was desperately waving her arm to flag them down. She was naked except for a thin skirt, and despite her horrific injuries, she managed to rasp out through scorched vocal cords: "Help me. I'm Suzanne Capper."

The motorists wrapped her shivering body in a jacket and called for an ambulance. Before losing consciousness, Suzanne made sure they knew exactly who had done this to her, naming each of her tormentors: "Bernadette, Jean, Glyn, Cliff, Jeff, and Anthony."

Suzanne Capper was sixteen years old. She had third-degree burns over eighty percent of her body, and doctors were astounded that she was still alive. But Suzanne was determined to tell her story—to ensure that the people who had kidnapped her, tortured her for a week, and set her on fire would not escape justice.

Four days later, despite the best efforts of medical staff, Suzanne Capper died from multiple organ failure. However, she had lived just long enough to identify her killers and set in motion a murder investigation that would uncover one of the most sadistic crimes in British history.

Suzanne Jane Capper was born in 1976 and grew up on Manchester's east side. Her early life was marked by instability. Her biological father left before she was born, and her mother, Elizabeth, struggled to provide a stable home. When Elizabeth's second marriage dissolved, fourteen-year-old Suzanne was briefly placed in local government care, feeling effectively abandoned.

Those who knew Suzanne described her as a gentle, timid girl desperate for acceptance. By her mid-teens, Suzanne had begun skipping school and drifting, seeking friendship wherever she could.

Unfortunately, her search for connection led her to the door of twenty-six-year-old Jean Powell's home on Langworthy

Road in Moston. Jean was a single mother of three young children, and Suzanne sometimes babysat for her and even stayed overnight. To Suzanne, this arrangement provided the semblance of friendship and family she desperately craved.

What Suzanne didn't realize was that Powell's home was a hub for petty criminals and drug users. Living there, along with Jean and her kids, was twenty-four-year-old Bernadette McNeilly and her children. Jean's younger brother, eighteen-year-old Clifford Pook, and Bernadette's teenage boyfriend, sixteen-year-old Anthony Dudson, were frequent visitors. Jeffrey Leigh, a twenty-six-year-old ex-convict, also stopped by often to buy or use amphetamines. Finally, Jean's estranged husband, twenty-nine-year-old Glyn Powell, was another regular visitor.

This motley crew of adults and teenagers was essentially the only group of friends Suzanne had. In August 1992, alarmed by the "evil new friends" gathering at Powell's home, Suzanne's older sister Michelle moved out of the neighborhood. Suzanne, however, continued to spend time at the house on Langworthy Road, perhaps too naïve to recognize the danger.

By early December 1992, several trivial resentments toward Suzanne had festered within the Powell/McNeilly circle. Jean Powell had recently accused Suzanne of trying to push her into an unwanted sexual encounter with a man the group referred to as "the Arab." In late November, Jean and Suzanne had met a man named Mohammed Yussif in the town of Sale. He had allegedly propositioned Jean, and she later claimed that Suzanne had "tried to make me go with an Arab."

Around the same time, Bernadette McNeilly and Anthony Dudson had contracted pubic lice, which they concluded "had been caught from Suzanne," who often slept in their bed at the house. They seethed at her over this embarrassment. On top of it all, Bernadette also believed that Suzanne had stolen a pink coat worth £50 that belonged to her.

These absurdly small slights—a rejected sexual advance, a case of lice, and a missing coat—coalesced into a motive for revenge.

On December 7, 1992, Jean Powell and Bernadette McNeilly decided to act on their grudges. They showed up at the house of Suzanne's stepfather, where Suzanne was then living, and told her that a boy she had a crush on was at Powell's home and wanted to see her. This was a lie designed to lure out the love-struck teenager.

Suzanne went willingly with Jean and Bernadette, but when she stepped through the door at 97 Langworthy Road, the trap sprang. There was no boy waiting—instead, Anthony Dudson and Glyn Powell immediately ambushed Suzanne.

Almost as soon as she arrived, the group struck Suzanne with brute force. She was punched and beaten viciously and knocked to the floor. At one point, they struck her with a large wooden instrument—a three-foot-long wooden fork—as a weapon. They pinned the terrified girl down and crudely hacked off her long brown hair, even shaving her head and eyebrows completely bald.

After this initial beating and head-shaving, they stripped Suzanne naked to humiliate her further. Bruised, shorn, and terrified, she was then shoved into a narrow cupboard under the stairs. The group jammed the door shut, locking Suzanne in a dark closet overnight on December 7.

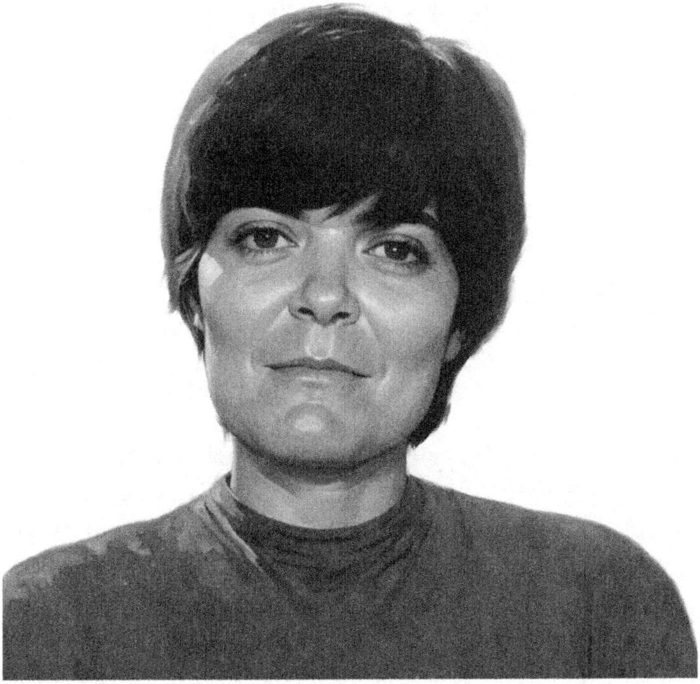

Bernadette McNeilly

The next day, her captors dragged her out and moved her to a different location to continue the abuse. They decided to use the house next door—91 Langworthy Road, which happened to be Bernadette McNeilly's former residence, and she still possessed a key. David Hill was the current resident at 91 Langworthy Road, but he lived alone and was acquainted with the group. They effectively took over his home for their gruesome purposes, and he was too intimidated to stop them.

In an upstairs bedroom, they bound Suzanne to an old bed frame so she could scarcely move. They tied her wrists and ankles with a cruel assortment of ligatures—cords, ropes, electrical cables, belts, even chains. Anything they could find to secure her limbs to the metal bed base. They also gagged her. In one instance, they shoved socks in her mouth and secured them in place so that her screams and pleas would be muffled.

What followed was seven days of systematic torture that would shock investigators. The group transformed into a gang of sadists, taking turns inflicting pain on the bound girl. They treated Suzanne not as a human being but as a plaything against which they could vent their rage and twisted urges.

From the outset, Bernadette McNeilly, in particular, took a leading role in tormenting Suzanne. What disturbed investigators and later the jury was how McNeilly didn't just participate in the torture; she transformed herself into a character to do it. At various points, McNeilly donned a creepy persona inspired by Chucky, the demonic doll from the horror film Child's Play. The group had in their possession an audio cassette with lines from the movie, and they played one line over and over through headphones placed on Suzanne's head: "I'm Chucky. Wanna play?"

McNeilly announced "Chucky's coming to play" at the start of each torture session, mocking Suzanne's terror. At times, Bernadette would lean in close to the helpless girl and hiss, "Chucky wants to play," while injecting her with drugs. Jean Powell later testified that McNeilly assumed the character of Chucky as she filled a syringe with amphetamine and jabbed it into Suzanne's arm. This ritualistic adoption of a sadistic fictional character revealed a disturbing psychological element that court psychiatrists later noted showed McNeilly wasn't just participating in violence. Rather, she was relishing a role that allowed her to detach from reality and her own humanity while inflicting pain.

Physical torture was constant and varied. The group beat Suzanne repeatedly with their fists and objects. At one point, they scrubbed her entire body with harsh, concentrated disinfectant and a stiff yard-bristle brush supposedly to "cleanse" her of the lice and filth. In truth, it was just to cause agonizing pain. They dumped undiluted household detergent and cleaning fluids into a bathtub and forced the girl into the caustic solution, scouring her raw skin. Her captors also burned her—a deep burn mark was seared between Suzanne's eyes, likely from someone stubbing out a cigarette on her face.

One of the most grotesque tortures involved pulling out Suzanne's teeth. Toward the end of her week in captivity, two of her front teeth were crudely extracted with pliers. This was done not only to cause excruciating pain but also with cold-blooded premeditation. The sadistic group was already planning to kill her, and by removing her teeth, they hoped to hinder the identification of her body. After yanking out her teeth, they laughed, saying that now she would be harder to recognize.

Through all of this, Suzanne's pleas and cries were largely silenced by the gag in her mouth. However, at times, her muffled screams could still be heard. David Hill later admitted he heard a female voice crying for help from the room. Paralyzed by fear of the violent gang, Hill did not rescue her.

By December 13, the group's energy for torment began to wane. They had to decide what to ultimately do with their victim. Suzanne was in awful condition: badly injured, weakened, and now a dangerous witness to their crimes if let go. On the seventh day of her captivity, the sadists formed a plan to commit murder.

In the early hours of December 14, 1992, Suzanne Capper's captors prepared to execute her. They untied her battered body from the bed and forced her into the trunk of a stolen white Fiat Panda. In the pre-dawn darkness, Glyn Powell drove out of Moston with his estranged wife, Jean Powell, as well as Bernadette McNeilly and Anthony Dudson. Suzanne lay crammed in the trunk, critically injured and likely drifting in and out of consciousness.

They drove thirteen miles to Werneth Low, a desolate hill and wooded area near Romiley in Stockport. At approximately 5:00 a.m., they arrived at a wooded stretch of remote land. The group dragged Suzanne out of the car and down an embankment, through thick brambles and brush on the hillside. She was so weak that she could barely stand or walk, so Glyn Powell and Anthony Dudson pushed her through the thorny undergrowth about forty yards from the road, where they dumped her on the cold ground.

Bernadette McNeilly had brought along a four-liter plastic canister filled with gasoline. In a final, macabre act, McNeilly doused Suzanne from head to toe with gasoline as she lay helpless in the grass. The group then stepped back for the final horrific act.

Later, each of the four would try to blame one of the others for what came next, but whoever it was, one of them pulled out a lighter. The testimony at trial varied significantly on this crucial point. According to some accounts, it was Glyn Powell who flicked the lighter first, while others claimed it was Dudson. McNeilly insisted she only poured the gasoline but didn't light it. The first attempt to ignite the gas failed, so someone tried again. In that confusing moment of finger-pointing and shared culpability, one of them deliberately set Suzanne on fire.

In an instant, Suzanne's gasoline-soaked body erupted into flames. The group watched as their victim burned alive, thrashing in the inferno. Her skin blistered and blackened; the fire was so intense that it caused severe burns to over eighty percent of her body.

Satisfied that their heinous task was done, the four murderers turned and headed back to their car, leaving Suzanne for dead. As they drove away from the scene, they did something almost as unfathomable as the act itself: They laughed and broke into song. Glyn Powell, Jean Powell, Bernadette McNeilly, and Anthony Dudson actually sang "Burn, baby, burn!" (the chorus from the song "Disco Inferno") as they departed.

Unbelievably, Suzanne Capper was not yet dead. After they left, Suzanne somehow clung to life. Engulfed in flames, she had rolled downhill. Perhaps the cold, wet winter ground helped douse the fire, or perhaps sheer willpower kept her alive a few minutes longer.

Once the flames subsided, Suzanne, horribly injured but still conscious, staggered through the woods. Incredibly, she managed to drag herself back up the embankment and onto a small rural lane sometime after the car had gone.

Around 6:30 a.m., two men driving along that quiet lane spotted her stumbling toward the road.

An ambulance was called, and she was rushed to the Burns Unit at Withington Hospital in south Manchester. Doctors were astonished to find Suzanne alive. In the burn unit, Suzanne remained conscious and coherent for several hours, and police officers were even able to interview her briefly despite her condition.

Suzanne recounted the nightmare she had been through over the past week. She not only identified her attackers by name, but she even gave the exact address—97 Langworthy Road—of where it had happened.

Despite the best efforts of the burn unit, Suzanne's injuries were too extensive. Four days after she was set ablaze, Suzanne Capper died at Withington Hospital on December 18, 1992, with her mother and sister by her bedside. She was just sixteen years old.

Greater Manchester Police, armed with the information Suzanne provided, acted swiftly on December 14, 1992. Just hours after Suzanne was found, police raided the house at 97 Langworthy Road in Moston at approximately 7:30 a.m. Jean Powell, Bernadette McNeilly, Glyn Powell, Jeffrey Leigh, and Clifford Pook were all present and promptly arrested. Anthony Dudson was picked up shortly thereafter.

The crime scenes themselves—both 97 and 91 Langworthy Road—yielded a trove of forensic and physical evidence corroborating Suzanne's account. In the upstairs bedroom at number 91, investigators found the makeshift restraints still attached to the bed: lengths of rope, electrical cords, and belts secured to the bed frame where Suzanne had been tied.

The floor and mattress were stained with blood, and clumps of Suzanne's hair were still scattered throughout the house. Police recovered the pliers that had been used to extract her teeth, with blood traces matching Suzanne's. One of her missing front teeth was discovered nearby.

At number 97, officers found the cupboard under the stairs where Suzanne had been imprisoned that first night—scratch marks and a few hairs inside attested to her desperate confinement there.

Investigators also seized the audio cassette tape that had been continuously playing the phrase "I'm Chucky, wanna play?" through headphones in the torture room. This tape was still in a cassette player, set to loop.

Physical evidence from outside the house also mounted. The Fiat Panda used to drive Suzanne to Werneth Low was found abandoned not far from the Powell residence. Forensic technicians matched tire tracks and trampled vegetation at the Werneth Low site to that vehicle and the suspects. Bits of melted plastic from a gas can were recovered from the burn site.

When confronted with the overwhelming evidence and Suzanne's dying testimony, the suspects began to turn on each other almost immediately. In police interviews and later in court, each tried to minimize their own role while pointing fingers at their accomplices.

By the time all evidence was gathered, the Crown Prosecution Service had prepared an extensive list of charges. In early 1993, murder charges were filed against Jean Powell, Glyn Powell, Bernadette McNeilly, Anthony

Dudson, Clifford Pook, and Jeffrey Leigh. Additional charges included false imprisonment, conspiracy to cause grievous bodily harm, and attempted murder. The stage was set for a major trial that fall.

The trial of Suzanne Capper's killers opened on November 16, 1993, at Manchester Crown Court. In the dock were five defendants: Jean Powell (26), Bernadette McNeilly (24), Glyn Powell (29), Anthony Dudson (17), and Jeffrey Leigh (27), all charged with murder and other counts. The sixth person, Clifford Pook, was also in the courtroom, but partway through the proceedings, the judge directed the jury to formally acquit Pook of murder due to insufficient evidence of his intent in the killing.

The trial lasted twenty-two days, during which time the gruesome evidence reduced jurors to tears. Most harrowing of all, the jury listened to Suzanne's own deathbed statement, which was read into evidence: a calm, heartbreaking account of what each of the accused had done to her.

The jurors also saw photographs of the injuries Suzanne suffered and saw items like the charred brush and blood-stained bed frame recovered from the crime scene. Physical exhibits such as the "Chucky" tape were played in court, sending chills down the spines of those present.

One by one, the defendants took the stand in their own defense—except Bernadette McNeilly, who chose not to testify. Their testimonies largely mirrored what they had told the police, with each minimizing responsibility.

On December 16, 1993, after ten hours of deliberation, the jury returned with their verdicts. Jean Powell, Bernadette

McNeilly, and Glyn Powell were each found guilty of murder and other associated charges beyond any doubt. Anthony Dudson was also found guilty of murder despite his youth and his protests that he hadn't lit the fire.

Jeffrey Leigh, however, was acquitted of murder—the jury was not convinced that Leigh had intended or directly assisted in killing Suzanne. He was instead convicted of false imprisonment. Clifford Pook had already pleaded guilty to conspiracy to cause grievous bodily harm and false imprisonment.

The next day, December 17, 1993, Justice Potts pronounced sentences. His words in court were scathing. He said their actions had been "as appalling a murder as it is possible to imagine," emphasizing how they had tortured Suzanne for their own amusement and revenge, displaying cruelty beyond belief.

Jean Powell, Glyn Powell, and Bernadette McNeilly were each sentenced to life in prison for the murder of Suzanne Capper. The judge imposed a minimum sentence of twenty-five years. Anthony Dudson, being legally a juvenile, was ordered to be detained at Her Majesty's Pleasure—an indefinite sentence for young offenders convicted of murder. The judge set a minimum tariff of eighteen years for Dudson.

Clifford Pook was sentenced to fifteen years for his admitted role in the conspiracy to cause grievous bodily harm. Jeffrey Leigh was sentenced to twelve years in prison for false imprisonment.

As the sentences were announced, there was a sense in the courtroom that justice had been served, albeit for a crime almost too horrific for justice to encompass. Suzanne's mother and family reportedly expressed satisfaction that the murderers would "never see daylight for a long time."

News of the Suzanne Capper case sent shockwaves through the community and the country. Many struggled to comprehend how a group of relatively ordinary young people could commit acts reminiscent of a horror movie. Some investigators stated that "for sheer mindless brutality," this crime ranked alongside the Moors Murders committed by Ian Brady and Myra Hindley in the 1960s.

Headlines highlighted the utter senselessness of the motive, emphasizing how trivial the reasons were for such monstrous behavior. The public struggled with that notion—that a teen girl could be burned alive over lice and a borrowed coat.

In Manchester, Suzanne's murder prompted some introspection about social services and community interventions. How did a sixteen-year-old essentially slip through every safety net—school, social workers, neighbors—to end up in this deadly situation?

In the years following the trial, the perpetrators served their sentences, and the question of their possible release became a contentious issue. Suzanne's mother, Elizabeth Dunbar, remained an outspoken advocate for keeping the killers behind bars, along with local MP Graham Stringer.

Despite these efforts, over time, one perpetrator after another gained parole:

• Jeffrey Leigh was released in 1998.

• Clifford Pook was freed in 2001.

• Anthony Dudson was released in 2013 at the age of thirty-seven.

• Bernadette McNeilly was released in 2015 after serving only twenty-two years.

• Jean Powell was released in 2017 at the age of fifty.

• Glyn Powell, the last of the convicted murderers still behind bars, was reportedly slated for release in 2023.

Each release was met with disbelief and outrage from those who remembered the case. How could a justice system allow a group of killers who spent a week torturing a sixteen-year-old girl, then set her on fire while she was still alive, to ever walk free?

And yet, one by one, they did. As one headline bluntly captured it: "Gang who tortured and killed tragic teen all set to be released from prison." The very idea that such cruelty has a time limit defies reason.

The Suzanne Capper case remains one of the most harrowing in modern British history. Her final act of bravery—identifying her killers with her dying breath—ensured they were brought to justice. But justice in Britain, it seems, has an expiration date. That anyone involved in such a sadistic, prolonged campaign of abuse could one day be deemed fit for release is not just troubling: it's shameful. What happened inside the house on Langworthy Road should have meant life behind bars, no exceptions. Instead, it stands as a haunting example of a system more concerned with rehabilitation than remembrance.

CHAPTER 3
THE PIZZA BOMBER

On a warm summer afternoon in Erie, Pennsylvania, television cameras captured what would become one of the most bizarre criminal cases in American history. Police officers surrounded a man sitting cross-legged on the pavement of a shopping center parking lot, his hands cuffed behind his back. Around his neck hung a strange, bulky device that resembled a homemade bomb. The officers maintained their distance as the man pleaded with them.

“I'm not lying,” he begged. “I'm not doing this because I want to. I'm doing this because I have to.”

For twenty-five minutes, news crews filmed as the man explained that someone had placed the device around his neck and forced him to rob a bank. Then, without warning, a shrill beeping sound emanated from the collar. The noise intensified, growing louder and faster.

“It's gonna go off!” the man cried just seconds before the device exploded.

As officers dove for cover, the man slumped forward, a gaping wound in his chest. The bomb squad, which had been summoned only minutes earlier, arrived too late. By the time they reached the scene, Brian Wells was already dead.

The date was August 28, 2003, and investigators were about to uncover one of the most elaborate and sinister criminal plots ever conceived—a deadly scavenger hunt, a group of twisted masterminds, and a pizza deliveryman caught in the middle.

Brian Douglas Wells was a quiet, unassuming man. At forty-six, he had been delivering pizzas for Mama Mia's Pizzeria for nearly a decade. His neighbors described him as trusting and kind. Certainly not the type to plan a bank heist.

That Thursday afternoon seemed routine when Wells left the pizza shop to make a delivery to an address near a remote television transmission tower on the outskirts of town. What happened during that delivery remains partially shrouded in mystery, but what is known is that at approximately 2:20 p.m., Wells walked into a PNC Bank branch in Millcreek Township, a suburb of Erie.

Bank surveillance footage showed Wells approaching the teller with an unusual calm, considering what he was about to do. He wore a plain white t-shirt with the brand name "Guess" printed across the front, under which a strange, boxy device protruded from his chest. In his hand, he carried what appeared to be a cane, though investigators later discovered it was actually a sawed-off shotgun that had been cleverly disguised. Wells slid a handwritten note across the counter.

The note was direct: He demanded $250,000. When the teller informed him she couldn't access that amount of money, he calmly accepted all the cash she could provide from her drawer—$8,702. Wells then walked out of the bank, sucking on a lollipop that had been given to him by his captors.

His strange demeanor caught the attention of a customer who followed him outside and jotted down his license plate number as Wells drove away in his car.

By 2:38 p.m., state troopers had spotted Wells in a parking lot near the bank. He was sitting outside his vehicle when officers approached with weapons drawn. They ordered him to the ground and handcuffed him. It was then that Wells began to plead with the officers.

"I don't have a lot of time," he said. "I'm not lying. I've been held hostage by people who had guns. There's a bomb around my neck."

With those words, the officers, following protocol for bomb threats, backed away and called for the bomb squad. Television news crews that had been monitoring police radio traffic arrived and began filming the scene. Wells sat cross-legged on the pavement, repeatedly asking officers to call his boss at the pizza shop—perhaps to verify his identity, or maybe to establish his role as a deliveryman.

At 3:18 p.m., with the bomb squad still en route, the device around Wells's neck began to beep. The sound quickened like a countdown, and before officers could react, it detonated. The explosion was powerful enough to tear a hole through Wells's chest, killing him instantly.

Inside Wells's car, investigators found several handwritten pages of instructions. It became clear that this was no ordinary bank robbery; it was the beginning of what investigators would come to call "a twisted treasure hunt."

The notes found in Wells's car revealed an elaborate scheme. They were addressed to the "Bomb Hostage" and contained detailed instructions for an elaborate scavenger hunt. After robbing the bank, Wells was supposed to follow a specific route to multiple locations around Erie. At each stop, he would find clues leading to keys or combination codes that would supposedly disarm the bomb around his neck.

Brian Wells

The first clue directed him to a McDonald's drive-thru, where a rock in a flowerbed concealed the next instruction. Other clues would lead him into the woods, where notes were taped under stones or hidden in jars. Investigators followed the trail and discovered several of these hidden messages, although some locations were empty, suggesting the perpetrators may have removed evidence after Wells's death.

The collar bomb itself was unlike anything law enforcement had ever seen. Constructed of metal, it had four padlocks and a three-digit combination lock. Inside the metal casing were two pipe bombs powered by commercial-grade smokeless powder. The device had been wired with three timers—two kitchen timers and one electronic timer—and included fake wiring and decoy stickers to confuse anyone attempting to disarm it.

Forensic analysis later revealed the bomb had been expertly crafted. It included sophisticated anti-tampering mechanisms that would trigger detonation if anyone attempted to remove it. The device was, in essence, a deadly puzzle with no solution.

The cane-shotgun found with Wells was equally sophisticated—a sawed-off shotgun disguised as a walking cane. The level of craftsmanship suggested that someone with mechanical expertise had built these devices.

As investigators pieced together the crime, they faced a central question: Was Brian Wells a willing participant in the robbery, or was he an innocent victim forced into a deadly game?

At the scene of his death, Wells had insisted he had been forced to rob the bank. He claimed that during his pizza delivery, armed men had ambushed him and locked the bomb around his neck. His final words to the police supported this narrative. He seemed genuinely frightened and repeatedly asked officers to help him.

Wells had no criminal record. His co-workers and neighbors described him as a timid, non-confrontational man who lived a modest life. Family members staunchly maintained that Brian would never willingly participate in a robbery.

However, as the investigation progressed, evidence emerged suggesting a more complicated story. The bomb's design was too sophisticated for Wells to remove on his own, but the timeline of events raised questions. The scavenger hunt was so elaborate that it would have been impossible to complete within the timeframe of the bomb's detonation. This led some investigators to believe Wells may have had prior knowledge of the plan, only to be double-crossed when he discovered the bomb was real.

Additionally, the "Guess" t-shirt Wells wore during the robbery was not his own. Some investigators speculated this might have been a cruel joke from the perpetrators—a taunt meaning "Guess who is behind this?" This level of sadistic calculation pointed to one or multiple minds far more twisted than Wells's friends and family believed him capable of.

On September 20, 2003, less than a month after the Wells incident, police received a bizarre letter. The handwritten note began, "This has nothing to do with the Wells case." The author, Bill Rothstein, went on to confess that there was a body in a freezer at his home.

When officers arrived at the address, they found William "Bill" Rothstein, a heavyset man with a long beard. True to the letter, police discovered the frozen body of James Roden in a chest freezer in Rothstein's garage.

Rothstein explained that he hadn't killed Roden—his ex-fiancée had. He claimed he was only helping to hide the body. The woman's name was Marjorie Diehl-Armstrong, and her connection to Rothstein would ultimately lead investigators to unravelling the pizza bomber case.

Marjorie Diehl-Armstrong was a study in contradictions. A former high school valedictorian with a master's degree, she possessed remarkable intelligence. Yet, by 2003, her life had spiraled into chaos. Her home was filled with thousands of pounds of rotting food and garbage—evidence of severe mental illness that included hoarding behaviors.

She also had a violent history. In 1984, she had shot a previous boyfriend but was acquitted on self-defense grounds. Her husband had died of a cerebral hemorrhage in 1992, ruled an accident at the time. And now, it seemed, she had killed James Roden, her latest boyfriend.

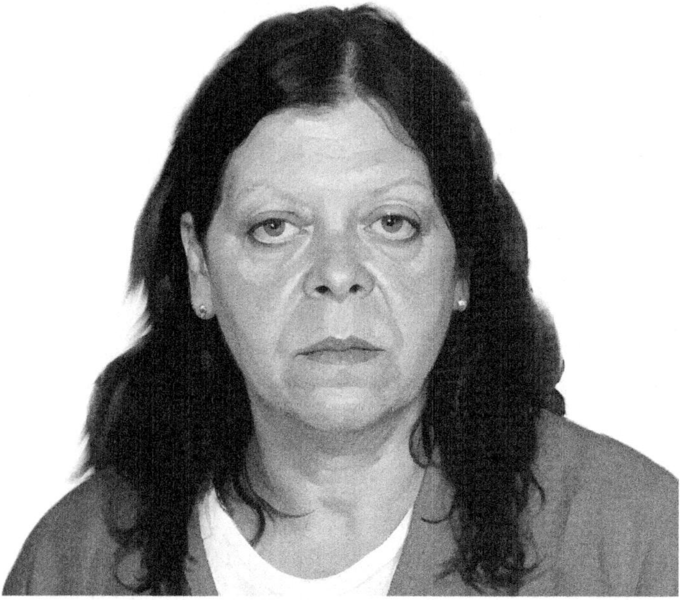

Marjorie Diehl-Armstrong

When questioned about Roden's death, Diehl-Armstrong admitted to shooting him during an argument. She eventually pleaded guilty but mentally ill to third-degree murder and was sentenced to seven to twenty years in prison.

As investigators explored the connection between Rothstein and Diehl-Armstrong, they began to suspect that these two eccentric individuals might have been involved in the Wells case, despite Rothstein's disclaimer in his letter.

Over the next four years, FBI agents conducted a meticulous investigation. They interviewed approximately 1,000 witnesses, analyzed every component of the bomb, and scrutinized the relationships between a growing cast of suspicious characters.

A break in the case came when investigators discovered that Diehl-Armstrong had provided kitchen timers to Rothstein —timers that matched those used in the collar bomb. Phone records showed she had been in contact with another man, Kenneth Barnes, about building explosive devices in the weeks before the bank robbery.

Barnes, a drug addict and friend of Diehl-Armstrong, eventually became a key witness. When arrested, he confessed that he had acted as a lookout during the bank robbery. According to Barnes, the original plan was for Wells to rob the bank with a fake bomb, but at the last minute, they switched it to a real one.

Barnes claimed that when Wells realized the bomb was real, he tried to back out. That's when another conspirator, Floyd Stockton—a roommate of Rothstein—allegedly pulled out a gun and forced Wells to go through with the robbery.

The puzzle pieces were falling into place. Investigators believed Diehl-Armstrong was the mastermind, motivated by a desire to secure money to hire Barnes to kill her father for inheritance. Rothstein, her former fiancée and a skilled handyman, had likely built the bomb using the timers she'd provided. Barnes served as a lookout during the robbery, while Stockton had helped secure the bomb around Wells's neck.

In July 2007, federal prosecutors announced an indictment against Diehl-Armstrong and Barnes for their roles in the deadly bank robbery. By this time, Rothstein had died of lymphoma in July 2004, never having been charged in the

Wells case. Finally, Stockton received immunity in exchange for his testimony.

Barnes pleaded guilty in September 2008 to conspiracy and using a destructive device in a crime of violence. He was sentenced to forty-five years in federal prison.

Diehl-Armstrong's case moved more slowly. She was initially declared mentally incompetent to stand trial but later deemed fit to face charges. Throughout pretrial hearings, she maintained her innocence and blamed Rothstein for masterminding the plot.

In October 2010, Diehl-Armstrong's trial began. Prosecutors presented physical evidence linking her to the crime, including her purchase of the timers used in the bomb. Barnes testified against her, detailing meetings in which she discussed killing her father and using the bank robbery proceeds to pay for the hit.

The prosecution portrayed Diehl-Armstrong as a cold, calculating criminal who orchestrated the entire scheme. Her defense argued that she was mentally ill and incapable of planning such an elaborate crime.

On November 1, 2010, a federal jury found Marjorie Diehl-Armstrong guilty on all charges: conspiracy to commit armed bank robbery, armed bank robbery resulting in death, and using a destructive device in a crime of violence. In February 2011, she was sentenced to life in prison plus thirty years.

To her dying day, Diehl-Armstrong maintained her innocence in the Wells case, insisting that Rothstein was the true mastermind. She died of breast cancer in prison in April 2017 at the age of sixty-eight.

Barnes died in prison of liver cancer in June 2019. Stockton, who received immunity, has remained out of the public eye.

As the full story emerged, investigators were struck by the bizarre nature of the conspirators. A federal prosecutor described them as "a group of twisted, intellectually bright, dysfunctional individuals who outsmarted themselves."

Marjorie Diehl-Armstrong was perhaps the most complex. Despite her brilliant mind, she suffered from severe mental illness. Psychiatrists diagnosed her with bipolar disorder and narcissistic personality traits, documented in court records. She was described as manipulative, hostile, and grandiose, displaying a fear of abandonment and an inflated sense of her own intelligence. Her hoarding was so extreme that investigators found over 4,000 pounds of rotting food in her home.

William Rothstein was equally strange—a reclusive handyman who spoke multiple languages and had the mechanical skills to build sophisticated devices. Friends described him as meticulous and obsessive. Like Diehl-Armstrong, he was a hoarder, though his compulsion centered on tools and gadgets rather than food.

Kenneth Barnes was characterized by investigators as "brain-fried from drugs." His judgment was impaired by years of substance abuse, yet he was trusted with a significant role in the conspiracy.

Floyd Stockton, a convicted sex offender, was the man who allegedly forced the collar bomb onto Wells's neck. His full role remains somewhat mysterious, as he was granted immunity and has stayed out of public view since.

These four individuals, each damaged in their own way, came together to create one of the most bizarre crimes in American history. Their plot combined elements of hostage-taking, bank robbery, and cruel manipulation into a deadly game that claimed an innocent life.

Though the conspirators were eventually brought to justice, Brian Wells's family has continued to fight to clear his name. His sister, Jean Heid, has maintained for years that her brother was an innocent victim, not a willing participant in the robbery.

Federal prosecutors, however, have stated that Wells was aware of the bank robbery plan, though they believe he was told the bomb would be fake. According to their theory, Wells only became a true victim when he realized the bomb was real and was forced to go through with the robbery at gunpoint.

This characterization of Wells as partially complicit has been a source of pain for his family. Without Wells alive to tell his side of the story, the full truth may never be known.

Even after the convictions, several aspects of the case remain mysterious.

The elaborate scavenger hunt raises questions. Why create such a complex scheme when the timers on the bomb made it virtually impossible for Wells to complete it? Was it merely a cruel joke, or was there something else at play?

The true mastermind remains debated. Though Diehl-Armstrong was convicted as the ringleader, some investigators believe Rothstein was the actual architect. His mechanical skills made him the likely bomb builder, and his subsequent death before charges could be filed means he "had the last laugh," as one investigator put it.

Wells's level of involvement remains a subject of controversy. Was he truly an innocent deliveryman caught in a deadly trap, or did he agree to participate in what he thought would be a nonviolent crime, only to be betrayed?

The "Guess" t-shirt Wells wore, which wasn't his, remains a strange detail. Was it indeed a taunt from the perpetrators, a sick joke embedded in their deadly game?

Finally, there's the question of why the crime was documented so thoroughly. The handwritten instructions, the bomb design, the scavenger hunt—all of it seems unnecessarily complex. Some have suggested that Rothstein, in particular, may have engineered the crime simply to prove he could, a display of perverted genius that ultimately cost an innocent man his life.

The Erie pizza bomber case stands out as one of the most bizarre criminal conspiracies in American history. It combined elements of psychological torture, mechanical ingenuity, and lethal calculation in ways that continue to disturb investigators.

The case also exposed the dangerous capabilities of damaged minds working in concert. Diehl-Armstrong's mental illness, Rothstein's mechanical genius, Barnes's desperation, and

Stockton's moral bankruptcy created a perfect storm that resulted in tragedy.

For law enforcement, the case represented a fact-finding challenge unlike any other. The seven-year investigation required extraordinary patience and attention to detail. FBI Special Agent Jerry Clark, who led the investigation, later called it one of the most complex cases of his career.

For the people of Erie, Pennsylvania, the case left a lingering shadow. The image of Brian Wells sitting on the pavement, pleading for his life moments before the collar bomb detonated, remains etched in the community's collective memory.

CHAPTER 4
THE REDRUM MURDER

Built in the 1700s, nestled between the lush forests of the Appalachian Mountains and the winding Schuylkill River, Reading, Pennsylvania, was a vibrant industrial city whose height of prosperity came during the railroad era. By the 1980s, however, the city had begun to fray around the edges as manufacturing declined.

In this working-class city of about 80,000 people, crime wasn't uncommon, but it typically consisted of petty thefts, bar fights, and the occasional domestic dispute. Violent crime existed, but rarely to the degree that it shocked the community. That changed dramatically in the summer of 1987, when a murder so gruesome and bizarre occurred that it sent shockwaves through the city and drew national attention.

On Saturday, July 25, 1987, David Lutz returned to his Fifth Street apartment around 3:30 a.m. after a night out partying. As he entered, he immediately knew something was terribly wrong. The apartment was eerily quiet, but evidence of violence was everywhere. Blood stained the carpet and walls. Trembling, he moved deeper into the apartment and discovered a sight so horrific that it would haunt him for years to come.

His roommate, forty-one-year-old Stanley Detweiler, lay on the floor, his body severed from his head. The decapitated head had been placed beside the body. Even more disturbing, someone had written the word "REDRUM"—"murder" spelled backward—on the wall in the victim's own blood. The killer had also scrawled "LSD" in blood on another wall.

Horror-struck and panicking, Lutz immediately called the police. When officers arrived, they were confronted with one of the most gruesome crime scenes any of them had ever seen. Reading Police Chief Rodney Steffy would later tell reporters, "What kind of lunatic would do something like this?"

The bloody writing on the wall provided an immediate, chilling clue. "REDRUM" was a direct reference to the horror film "The Shining," based on Stephen King's novel of the same name, which had coincidentally aired on television just a week before the murder. This suggested that whoever had committed this atrocity might have been inspired by fiction, blurring the lines between Hollywood horror and real-life terror.

Stanley Detweiler was not the type of person anyone would expect to fall victim to such violence. At forty-one, he was known throughout the community as a kind-hearted, gentle soul. He worked as a banquet setup staffer at a local Holiday Inn and played the organ at his church on Sundays.

Stanley, a talented pianist who sometimes tuned pianos for extra money, was described by those who knew him as generous to a fault—so much so that Stanley's good nature had occasionally placed him in risky situations before. On one occasion, he had picked up a hitchhiker who had repaid his kindness by threatening him with a knife and stealing his car.

Despite such experiences, Stanley remained trusting and quick to help others. He shared his Reading apartment with his younger roommate, David Lutz, and was looking forward to his forty-second birthday, which would have been just two days after his murder on July 27.

No one could have imagined that this gentle man would become the victim of one of the most brutal murders in Reading's history.

The events leading up to Stanley Detweiler's murder began innocently enough. On Friday evening, July 24, 1987, David Lutz went out partying in downtown Reading. While socializing on North 10th Street, twenty-year-old Lutz met sixteen-year-old Michael Boettlin Jr.

Lutz was attracted to the teenager and, hoping to impress him enough to continue the party back at his place, began boasting about his lifestyle. He told Boettlin that he and his roommate "had a lot of money and a nice stereo," and he even hinted that his roommate was wealthy and away on vacation. Lutz then invited Boettlin over to drink and party in private.

Initially, Boettlin agreed, and the two headed toward Lutz's home on South Fifth Street. But along the way, Boettlin changed his mind and decided to go to another party instead. Lutz, still hopeful, gave the teenager his address anyway in case he changed his mind before they parted ways.

What Lutz didn't realize was that his boastful comments had planted a seed in Michael Boettlin's mind—a tip about an apartment supposedly full of valuables and cash, sitting empty.

Shortly afterward, Boettlin ran into his old acquaintance, twenty-two-year-old John Calvaresi, at another party elsewhere in the city. Calvaresi had actually been Boettlin's babysitter years earlier, when the teen was just a child. Now, Calvaresi gladly bought beers for the underage Boettlin, and as they drank into the late hours, the conversation turned to making some quick money.

Boettlin mentioned the boast he'd heard from Lutz: a "rich roommate" and "fancy stereo system" in an apartment that should be unoccupied. Lutz had said his roommate was on vacation, and Boettlin assumed Lutz himself wouldn't be back until nearly 4:00 a.m.

Calvaresi, who was nearly broke and always up for mischief, thought it sounded like an easy score. The pair formed a plan to break in and rob the place that very night, never imagining how horrifically wrong things would go.

As Friday night passed into the early morning hours of Saturday, John Calvaresi and Michael Boettlin set out to burglarize the Fifth Street apartment. Around 2:00 a.m., they arrived at the address David Lutz had given Boettlin. The pair was confident the apartment would be empty. They planned for a quick smash-and-grab of electronics and cash with no one home to stop them.

Calvaresi and Boettlin forced their way in, kicking open the apartment's front door with a loud crash. However, the noise woke someone inside. To their surprise, Lutz's roommate, Stanley Detweiler, was home after all, asleep in his bed until the commotion roused him.

Startled and still groggy, Detweiler hurried toward the source of the sound only to come face-to-face with the two intruders. A struggle ensued in the doorway. Calvaresi, taller and stronger, lunged at Detweiler and tackled him to the floor. The panicked victim tried to fight back, but Boettlin joined in, repeatedly kicking Detweiler in the face as Calvaresi held him down.

Together, the attackers brutally beat the man until he lay unconscious, his body half in the doorway and half in the building's entryway. During the vicious beating, Detweiler suffered five broken ribs among other injuries. The intruders then dragged the unconscious victim fully inside and shut the door behind them.

Michael Boettlin

Breathing heavily after the struggle, the two regrouped. Calvaresi stalked off to the kitchen while Boettlin began searching the apartment for valuables. The ransacking proved disappointing; Lutz's boasts had been greatly exaggerated. The modest apartment held little of worth, and Boettlin found only a glass coin bank containing about $22 in quarters and a checkbook.

Meanwhile, Calvaresi emerged from the kitchen armed with a ten-inch butcher's knife. What happened next would turn a simple burglary into an almost unspeakable horror.

Returning to the living room where Detweiler lay unconscious, Calvaresi—perhaps fueled by adrenaline or twisted curiosity—posed a shocking question to his young accomplice: "Should I cut his head off?"

Boettlin, in a moment of sheer panic and confusion, gave a short reply that he would regret forever: "Okay." The naïve teenager didn't believe Calvaresi would actually do it; he was in shock and simply blurted out a response, terrified that if he protested, the volatile older man might turn on him next.

"I remember thinking, 'I don't know this guy. What if I'm next?'" Boettlin later recalled, insisting he was traumatized by what followed.

As Detweiler began to regain consciousness on the floor, John Calvaresi moved in with the knife. He pinned the victim down, kneeling on the man's chest, while Detweiler weakly tried to fight back in terror. To keep the victim subdued, Boettlin stepped on Detweiler's arm, holding him in place.

Then, in an act of unfathomable brutality, Calvaresi began sawing at Stanley Detweiler's neck with the kitchen knife. The blade wasn't very sharp. Calvaresi had to work at the grisly task, slicing back and forth until the neck was nearly cut through. Then, using his bare hands, he twisted and pulled until he tore the head free from the remaining tissue. When the gruesome deed was done, he set Detweiler's severed head beside the lifeless body on the living room floor.

The nightmare was not over. Spattered in blood, Calvaresi grabbed a towel to wipe himself off. In a disturbing flourish, he then dipped his fingers in the victim's blood and began writing on the walls. On the kitchen wall, he scrawled the word "REDRUM"—a direct reference to a key scene in "The Shining." Unsatisfied, Calvaresi told Boettlin to smear the bloody letters to obscure any fingerprints and then wrote the word "REDRUM" again on another wall, this time more clearly. He also daubed the letters "LSD" nearby, joking that LSD was his favorite drug; he thought adding it would make it more interesting for whoever found the scene.

John Calvaresi

Throughout the ordeal, Michael Boettlin stood by in a state of shock. By his later account, he was frozen and horrified by what his friend had done, yet too afraid to intervene. Having committed an atrocity, the pair hurried to cover their tracks. They made only a cursory attempt to collect loot, notably failing even to take cash from the victim's wallet in their haste. Before leaving, however, Calvaresi and Boettlin took the time to clean up in the bathroom, washing off the blood before they fled into the night.

News of the crime spread quickly through Reading, leaving residents in disbelief. The sheer brutality of Detweiler's murder—a beheading in a home invasion—made headlines and drew national attention. Local authorities were shaken. Berks County District Attorney George Yatron struggled to find words to describe the crime scene's grotesque nature.

The bizarre "REDRUM" message immediately caught media attention; reporters seized upon it for headlines, dubbing it the "REDRUM Murder." The fact that a Hollywood horror motif had been recreated in a Pennsylvania apartment was morbidly fascinating to the public.

Reading suddenly found itself in the spotlight for a grisly murder rather than its industrial past or the Reading Railroad of Monopoly fame. To a community already struggling with rising crime, the Detweiler case was something entirely different, described by some as perhaps the most vicious homicide in the city's modern history.

In quiet suburbs and city row homes alike, residents double-checked their locks that weekend. Rumors swirled about cults or madmen on the loose, given the almost ritualistic mutilation and messages in blood. Some even drew comparisons to the Manson family murders of nearly two decades earlier—violent crimes marked by similar blood-written messages and a feeling of senseless evil. At Detweiler's church, fellow congregants wept and tried to make sense of the loss of a good man in such an evil act.

Local newspapers ran front-page stories on the murder for days as police worked feverishly to identify the perpetrators.

From the outset, detectives faced intense pressure to solve the case. The crime scene itself, while horrifying, yielded valuable clues. Bloody shoeprints and fingerprints were left throughout the apartment. The vandalized walls suggested the killer might have been inspired by the media, pointing to a young or at least psychologically disturbed suspect.

Crucially, David Lutz provided investigators with their first lead. In his initial interview, still dazed by shock, Lutz had not mentioned his encounter with the teenage stranger the night before. However, as police pressed him about anyone who knew he would be out that night, Lutz recalled his conversation with "Michael"—how he had bragged about the apartment and given Michael the address. However, Lutz didn't know Michael's last name.

That fragment of information was enough for detectives to start canvassing the area where Lutz met the youth. They learned of the party that had taken place that Friday night and began interviewing attendees. In short order, one attendee recalled that Michael was accompanied by an adult man in his early twenties named John Calvaresi. Another witness knew Michael Boettlin from the neighborhood, and they were able to provide his full name and even an address for his family's home.

Separately, investigators heard from at least one of Boettlin's friends that the teen had been bragging about the crime after it happened. This was the final piece of the puzzle that investigators needed.

Just four days after Stanley Detweiler's murder, on July 29, 1987, authorities moved to arrest Michael Boettlin Jr. They descended on the Boettlin home, where the sixteen-year-old lived with his mother and stepfather. Boettlin was taken into custody without incident and promptly arraigned as an adult on an array of charges, including criminal homicide, first-degree murder, second-degree murder, voluntary manslaughter, burglary, robbery, aggravated assault, and conspiracy.

The very next day, police tracked down John Calvaresi. The twenty-two-year-old was arrested in a rural area outside Reading on July 30, 1987. He, too, was booked on identical charges.

News of the swift arrests reassured the rattled community of Reading. Locals were stunned to learn the ages of the suspects—one barely old enough to drive, the other just a young adult. Both suspects had ties to Reading's youth social scene, and the fact that a teenager was involved particularly troubled residents.

Meanwhile, prosecutors signaled they would pursue the most severe penalties available. Boettlin, though a minor, faced the grim prospect of life in prison—or even a possible death penalty—given the first-degree murder charge.

Legal proceedings began to unfold in two separate tracks for the co-defendants. John Calvaresi, the older ringleader and the one who had physically committed the beheading, decided early on to cooperate with prosecutors. In March 1988, Calvaresi pleaded guilty but mentally ill to first-degree murder. As part of his plea deal, he agreed to testify against

Michael Boettlin, effectively removing the possibility that Calvaresi himself might face the death penalty.

During his testimony, Calvaresi recounted the night of the murder in chilling detail, describing without emotion how he cut off Stanley Detweiler's head. Courtroom observers were struck by his flat, remorseless demeanor on the stand. Calvaresi attempted to explain his actions by pointing to his mental disturbances.

"There was something wrong because you just don't go around cutting people's heads off for nothing," he told the judge and jury.

A court-ordered psychiatric evaluation found that while Calvaresi did suffer from significant mental health issues, including epilepsy worsened by improper medication and drug abuse, he was legally sane and fit to stand trial. The diagnosis of "guilty but mentally ill" meant he would serve his sentence in state prison, albeit with access to psychiatric treatment. The judge accepted Calvaresi's plea and immediately imposed a sentence of life in prison for the first-degree murder, sparing him from execution.

With Calvaresi's fate sealed, attention turned to Michael Boettlin Jr.'s trial. Due to intense pretrial publicity in Berks County, the defense successfully moved for a change of venue. The trial was relocated across the state to Westmoreland County, Pennsylvania, in hopes of finding jurors who hadn't been tainted by the "REDRUM" media coverage.

In August 1988, one year after the crime, now seventeen-year-old Boettlin stood trial for murder before a Westmoreland County jury. Prosecutors presented a strong case, bolstered by physical evidence and, most damaging,

John Calvaresi's firsthand testimony. Calvaresi took the stand and recounted the crime, placing blame on Boettlin as an eager participant. He testified that Boettlin had not only kicked Detweiler during the initial assault but also consented to the beheading by uttering "Okay" when prompted.

Boettlin's defense sought to minimize the teen's role. They painted him as a frightened boy under the sway of a deranged older man. Boettlin didn't deny being present, but he claimed he never believed Calvaresi would actually kill Detweiler. On the stand, Boettlin expressed remorse and insisted he was paralyzed by fear once the violence began. The defense highlighted that Boettlin had no history of violent crime and didn't start the more brutal acts.

Ultimately, however, the gruesome facts were inescapable. An innocent man had been killed in the course of a robbery that Boettlin helped plan and execute. The jury also heard about the chilling blood-scrawled messages on the walls and other disturbing details that underscored the depravity of the crime scene.

After deliberating, the Westmoreland County jury delivered its verdict on August 15, 1988. Michael Boettlin Jr. was found guilty of first-degree murder, second-degree murder, felony murder during a robbery, and related offenses. The teen stood quietly, showing no emotion as the forewoman announced the guilty verdict on all counts.

Given the first-degree murder conviction, a mandatory life sentence was imposed, meaning that Boettlin, at seventeen years old, would spend the rest of his natural life behind bars with no chance of parole. In addition, the judge sentenced him to an extra term of twenty to forty years for the robbery, burglary, and conspiracy charges—to be served consecutively.

As Judge Calvin Smith delivered the sentence, he admonished Boettlin for his role in the savagery, emphasizing that youth was no excuse for such cruelty. Boettlin's family quietly wept in the courtroom while Detweiler's relatives nodded somberly, feeling that justice had been served.

John Calvaresi was a troubled twenty-two-year-old with a history of mental health issues when he committed the brutal murder. Diagnosed with epilepsy as a child, Calvaresi had been prescribed anti-seizure medications but often mixed them with alcohol and illegal drugs, causing violent mood swings and erratic behavior.

According to psychiatric testimony presented at his sentencing, Calvaresi had attempted suicide multiple times and experienced psychotic episodes. He had once written a threatening letter to President Ronald Reagan, prompting a Secret Service investigation. Friends described him as a high school dropout and drifter who rode motorcycles and shot pool around town, with little direction in his life.

Despite his rough edges, he had once served as a babysitter for young Michael Boettlin, who was six years his junior. This early connection would later prove fatal for Stanley Detweiler, as it brought together two individuals who never should have reconnected.

Michael Boettlin Jr. was just sixteen at the time of the murder and about to enter the tenth grade that fall. By all accounts, he was an ordinary teenager who enjoyed partying and was flattered by the attention of Calvaresi, who now treated him like an adult by buying him beer.

Boettlin's background offered few clues to explain his participation in such a heinous crime. He came from a working-class family and had no significant criminal history before the murder. What might have seemed like a thrilling adventure—breaking into an apartment with an older friend—spiraled into a nightmare beyond imagination.

In the decades following 1988, both convicted perpetrators remained behind bars in Pennsylvania's state prison system. However, their stories did not end at sentencing.

John Calvaresi, inmate FD-2494, was sent to serve his life term. He spent years in various prisons and, according to records, struggled with his health. On July 31, 2015, after twenty-eight years of incarceration, John Italo Calvaresi died of natural causes at age fifty.

Michael Boettlin Jr. remained in prison as well, serving his life sentence. As years passed, Boettlin reportedly matured and made efforts at rehabilitation. He earned his GED diploma in 1994 while incarcerated and became an avid reader of books and newspapers, trying to educate himself. By his mid-forties, Boettlin had spent well over half his life in prison and had a spotless disciplinary record.

His case, along with those of many other juvenile lifers, took on new significance in light of evolving legal standards. In 2012, the U.S. Supreme Court ruled in Miller v. Alabama that mandatory life-without-parole sentences for crimes committed by juveniles are unconstitutional. This landmark decision opened the door for Boettlin to receive a new sentence that would allow a chance at parole.

Under Pennsylvania court orders following Miller, Boettlin was granted a resentencing hearing in 2017. In October 2017, then-forty-six-year-old Michael Boettlin Jr. returned to a Berks County courtroom to face resentencing for the murder he had committed as a teenager three decades earlier. Family members of Stanley Detweiler were present, still haunted by the memory of their loved one's fate.

Boettlin, graying and soft-spoken, addressed the court and expressed deep remorse for his actions in 1987. He didn't attempt to excuse the crime, acknowledging that no apology could undo the harm. After considering factors of Boettlin's youth at the time of the crime and his prison record, Judge Paul Yatron issued a new sentence of forty years to life in state prison.

This meant that Boettlin would become eligible for parole after serving a total of forty years. Given the time he had already spent locked up since 1987, he will first be able to petition for release in 2027, when he will be fifty-six years old.

CHAPTER 5
A STRANGE CASE

The predawn air hung still over Louisville on Sunday, May 27, 1990. Most neighborhoods slumbered peacefully on what should have been an ordinary Memorial Day weekend.

But this would be no ordinary call for the firefighters racing toward South Ninth Street. Flames had engulfed an abandoned house, sending plumes of acrid smoke into the darkness. As they battled the blaze at 2907 S. Ninth St., none could have anticipated the nightmarish discovery that awaited them.

When the last embers were quenched, and after the smoke cleared, firefighters made a horrific find. Inside the charred ruins lay the headless, burned remains of a woman. Her body was so severely damaged by the flames that immediate identification was impossible. More disturbing still was the obvious absence of her head—a calculated attempt to thwart her identification and obscure a ghastly crime. Homicide detectives soon arrived at the scene, their faces grim as they surveyed what would become one of Louisville's most disturbing crime scenes in recent memory.

As news of the headless corpse spread through the community in the following hours, a palpable anxiety gripped the city. Who was this woman? What monster could have committed such a heinous act? While these questions hung in the air, detectives were already pursuing a crucial lead: a missing persons report filed for forty-four-year-old Kathleen Strange, a beloved schoolteacher who hadn't shown up for a planned family gathering that holiday weekend.

By Monday, a meticulous search yielded the most damning piece of evidence: Kathleen's severed head, buried in the vegetable garden behind her own home. A bullet from a thirty-eight-caliber revolver was lodged in her skull, revealing the grim truth that she had been executed before her body was mutilated and burned. The discovery shifted the focus of the investigation directly to Kathleen's home—and the man with whom she shared it: her husband, John Strange.

To understand the terrible fate that befell Kathleen Strange, one must first unravel the complex web of relationships within the Strange family. Kathleen was, by all accounts, a kind and compassionate woman who had touched many lives as a teacher. The petite forty-four-year-old had even taught Sunday school, earning the respect and admiration of colleagues and students alike.

Kathleen had been married once before, and from that prior relationship came her only child, Anthony Eugene "Tony" Jones, who was twenty-two years old in 1990. Tony had shown troubling signs of a violent streak in his youth, a foreshadowing of the darkness that would eventually consume him.

Her marriage to John Strange was relatively new, having wed two years earlier. At forty-seven, John was also an educator, teaching at a local Baptist school. Their union had created a blended family that included Kathleen's son Tony, as well as John's children from his previous marriage. Among them was twenty-year-old Christine Strange, who lived with her boyfriend, Sam Edwards, in Columbia, Kentucky, about two hours from Louisville.

On the surface, the Strange household appeared ordinary—two teachers building a quiet life together, their adult children establishing lives of their own. However, beneath this veneer of normalcy lay fault lines of tension and conflict. John and Kathleen's marriage had grown increasingly strained. As one acquaintance delicately put it, they "had their differences," though friends would later reveal that arguments had become commonplace. Financial pressures and disagreements about their children plagued the relationship, with whispers circulating that Kathleen had considered leaving John.

Tony Jones also harbored deep resentment toward his stepfather. Having dropped out of school, Tony drifted aimlessly, occasionally clashing with his mother about his lifestyle choices. In stark contrast stood Christine Strange, whose loyalty to her father was unwavering. Despite living two hours away, she maintained an intense bond with John, who had helped her and her boyfriend Sam establish themselves. Christine idolized her father, a devotion that would later prove pivotal in the aftermath of Kathleen's murder.

As Memorial Day weekend 1990 began, Kathleen Strange anticipated a welcome break from teaching and the chance to spend time with her family. She had spoken with relatives about gathering together, but by Saturday night, May 26, those plans took a horrific turn.

That Saturday evening, a confrontation erupted inside the Strange home. In the supposed safety of the couple's bedroom, Kathleen was shot execution-style at close range. The bullet entered the back of her head, killing her almost instantly.

What followed defies comprehension. Rather than calling for help, Kathleen's killer embarked on a cold, calculated cover-up. Her body was transported—likely under the cover of darkness—to the vacant house on Ninth Street. There, in that dilapidated building, the perpetrator decapitated her corpse with crude instruments, a ghastly act of mutilation intended to thwart identification. The head was carefully wrapped and kept separate (later to be buried in the garden at home), while her headless body was doused with an accelerant and set ablaze in the predawn hours of Sunday.

Shortly after midnight, a passerby noticed the flames and alerted the fire department. By the time firefighters arrived, portions of the old frame house were already engulfed. Upon extinguishing the fire, they then discovered the charred remains and immediately summoned police.

Investigators noted that the victim's clothing had been partially burned away, but some fabric remained. Despite the fire damage, it was evident that the body had been deliberately mutilated—the head and hands were also missing, suggesting a determined effort to prevent identification through dental records or fingerprints.

As Sunday wore on, John Strange told friends and police that Kathleen was missing. He claimed ignorance of her whereabouts, suggesting she might have gone out of town or been out late. What John failed to mention immediately was that he himself was suffering from burns on his arms and hands. He had spent part of Sunday being treated at a hospital for second-degree burns, which he explained away as an accident from a backyard barbecue grill. Of course, this explanation did little to convince detectives once they learned of it. The coincidence was too striking: a missing wife, a burned husband, and a headless body found in a fire.

By Monday, May 28—Memorial Day itself—suspicion centered squarely on John Strange. Investigators secured a search warrant for the Strange residence. In the backyard garden, under freshly turned soil, they made the crucial discovery of Kathleen's severed head wrapped in cloth. Inside the house, forensic teams detected traces of blood beneath the carpet and in the trunk of Kathleen's car. The evidence overwhelmingly indicated that Kathleen had been killed at home before her body was moved. Later that day, John R. Strange was arrested and charged with murder, abuse of a corpse, and arson.

In a shocking twist, police discovered that John had not acted alone in the aftermath of the murder—the investigation uncovered a family conspiracy to conceal the crime. Phone records and witness interviews placed Christine Strange and Sam Edwards at the Strange house in Louisville on the very weekend of the murder. Under questioning, both eventually admitted to helping John destroy evidence after Kathleen was killed. The two had driven from Columbia, possibly at John's urgent request, and arrived after Kathleen was already dead.

Christine and Sam were charged with tampering with physical evidence. They had washed Kathleen's blood-soaked clothing to eliminate forensic evidence and helped clean the crime scene, scrubbing bloodstains and removing any traces that might incriminate John. This calculated effort to erase evidence suggested prior planning and a clear state of mind after the murder. John had enlisted his own daughter and her boyfriend as a cleanup crew.

The notion of a daughter helping cover up the beheading and burning of her stepmother stunned investigators and the public alike. Christine was just twenty, perhaps under her father's powerful influence, while Sam, an outsider to the family, reportedly did whatever Christine asked. Both declined media interviews when their names surfaced, their exact motivations remaining unclear. Had John promised them something? Were they simply obeying him out of misguided loyalty or fear? The case had now ensnared multiple members of the Strange family in a web of criminal charges.

By early June 1990, John Strange awaited trial for his wife's murder. At a bond reduction hearing on June 28, he remained mostly silent, speaking through his attorney. Given the gruesome details and compelling evidence, the judge maintained his high bond. Christine Strange and Sam Edwards were also indicted on evidence-tampering charges. Investigators hoped one or both might cooperate in exchange for leniency, potentially providing a complete account of the plot to conceal Kathleen's murder.

In late August 1991, John R. Strange's murder trial began in a Louisville courtroom. The sensational details guaranteed intense media coverage, and the courthouse was packed with observers. The prosecution painted John as a cold-blooded killer who murdered his wife to escape a failing marriage and possibly claim life insurance—a motive suggested, though never fully substantiated. They presented the forensic evidence: The bullet retrieved from Kathleen's skull matched a revolver owned by John, blood spatter analysis from the Strange home matched Kathleen's blood type, and charred fabric from the burned body was consistent with a dress Kathleen had worn. Most damning was the discovery of Kathleen's head buried on John's property—something only the killer could have done. Prosecutors argued that John had killed Kathleen at home and then methodically carried out a plan to mutilate and burn her body to avoid detection.

Family drama played a crucial role in the proceedings. Christine Strange had struck a deal, agreeing to testify for the prosecution. In a tense courtroom moment, she admitted to helping her father clean up after the murder. "Daddy told me it was an accident at first," she testified softly, explaining that John had begged for her help. Christine detailed how she and Sam washed Kathleen's clothes and watched as her father loaded the body into Kathleen's car. Her testimony was a double-edged sword. While confirming John's cover-up, it also opened the door for the defense's radical new theory.

William Radigan, John's defense attorney, employed a stunning strategy. In his opening statement, he made a shocking admission and accusation: John had indeed decapitated and burned Kathleen's body, the lawyer conceded—but he hadn't killed her. Instead, Radigan told the jury that Kathleen's own son was the real murderer. Gasps rippled through the courtroom as Radigan clarified he meant Anthony "Tony" Jones, Kathleen's son from her previous marriage. According to the defense, Tony harbored deep animosity toward his mother and hatred for John. On that fateful night, the defense claimed, Tony came to the Strange house, argued with Kathleen, and shot her in the head. John supposedly discovered Kathleen's body after Tony fled. Fearing his stepson would be blamed, John panicked. In an irrational state, Radigan argued, John had decided to conceal the death by dismembering the corpse and setting the fire, hoping to make it appear as if an unknown assailant had killed Kathleen.

This claim—that a grieving husband would behead and burn his wife's body to protect the real killer—was met with obvious skepticism. Under cross-examination, John maintained, "I know how it looks, but I didn't kill Kathy." He described Tony and Kathleen's turbulent relationship, suggesting Tony might have snapped. However, there was no physical evidence placing Tony at the crime scene, and he had not been charged in connection with Kathleen's death. The prosecutor pointed out that John never called 911 upon supposedly finding his wife's body, nor did he seek medical help—instead, he embarked on a grotesque dismemberment and arson scheme. In a withering cross-examination, the prosecutor asked, "Mr. Strange, what kind of innocent man responds to his wife's murder by cutting off her head?" John had no compelling answer beyond claiming he was in shock and not thinking clearly.

Outside the jury's presence, observers noted that John remained emotionless throughout much of the trial, even when graphic forensic photos were displayed. If the defense hoped for sympathy by portraying John as a distraught protector of his stepson, it likely backfired.

After a two-week trial filled with forensic testimony, tearful statements from Kathleen's relatives, and the bizarre spectacle of the defendant essentially admitting to horrific acts while denying murder, the case went to the jury.

The verdict came swiftly. In September 1991, the jury found John R. Strange guilty on all counts: murder, abuse of a corpse, and first-degree arson. Citing the "exceptionally cruel and depraved" nature of the crime, the judge imposed a severe sentence: sixty-five years in prison. John showed little emotion as the sentence was read. Across the gallery, Kathleen's family members wept quietly, relieved that justice had been secured—at least partially.

Even as John Strange began serving his sentence, a question lingered: What about Tony Jones? John's trial had effectively accused him of matricide in open court. At the time, Tony was a free man; he had not been charged in connection with his mother's death and publicly denied any involvement. For a while, it seemed Tony might escape any legal consequences in the Strange case. However, Tony's own actions soon brought him infamy of a different sort.

On May 8, 1992, less than a year after John's conviction, Tony Jones committed a brutal murder that shocked Louisville anew. In Cherokee Park, a popular green space that also served as a meeting place for local gay men, Tony set out on what he chillingly described as "hunting queers." He lured thirty-six-year-old Richard Gilman into a secluded area and, in an act of hate-fueled violence, shot him to death simply because of the victim's sexual orientation. The crime was senseless and heinous—a hate crime before that term had fully entered public consciousness. Tony was quickly arrested, and Louisville prosecutors charged him with murder, seeking the death penalty for the now twenty-four-year-old.

The Richard Gilman murder trial in late 1992 dominated Louisville headlines. Not only was it a high-profile hate crime, but many noted the dark parallel: Tony was now on trial for a brutal murder just as his stepfather had been. The Strange family seemed cursed with violence. During Tony's trial, prosecutors revealed how he had bragged to acquaintances about hunting gay men in Cherokee Park. The evidence against him was overwhelming, and the jury convicted him of murder and related charges. While they stopped short of a death sentence, in October 1992, the court delivered an extraordinary punishment: Anthony "Tony" Jones was sentenced to 533 years in prison. This staggering number—essentially five centuries behind bars—sent a clear message, though news reports dryly noted that despite the massive sentence, Jones would be eligible for parole in ten years due to parole laws at the time. The jury, outraged at this possibility, publicly urged officials to deny him parole at every opportunity.

With Tony now a convicted murderer, law enforcement could not ignore the lingering questions about Kathleen Strange's death. John's defense accusations suddenly took on a different light. In December 1992, Louisville authorities announced they were reopening the investigation into Kathleen's murder, focusing on Tony's potential involvement. The community was stunned. Could both John and Tony have been involved in Kathleen's death?

Investigators reviewed old evidence and conducted new interviews. They looked for any indication that Tony might have been present during the Memorial Day 1990 crime.

Some witnesses recalled seeing an unfamiliar car near the Strange home that weekend—possibly Tony's. Meanwhile, a former friend of Tony's told police that Tony had once expressed hatred for his mother and even mused about "getting rid of her," though such secondhand remarks were difficult to verify. With Tony now behind bars, prosecutors convened a grand jury to hear evidence regarding his involvement in Kathleen's case.

By January 1993, a Jefferson County grand jury indicted Tony Jones for complicity in the murder of Kathleen Strange, accusing him of participating in or orchestrating the killing alongside John. Prosecuting Tony for Kathleen's death proved to be complex. John, unsurprisingly, refused to cooperate, given that implicating Tony might undermine his future appeals. Christine's testimony had placed only John at the scene after the fact, not Tony. Lacking direct evidence tying Tony to the actual shooting, the case was largely circumstantial. Nonetheless, prosecutors moved forward, determined to hold Tony accountable if he had any role in the crime.

In mid-1993, Tony Jones was brought to Louisville to be arraigned for Kathleen's murder. In a bitter irony, he appeared in the same courthouse where he had been convicted of the Cherokee Park murder months before. Tony, now twenty-five and already serving a life term, maintained an impassive demeanor. He pleaded not guilty and, through his attorney, dismissed the charges as "retaliation for what my stepfather said." It seemed Tony and John were pointing fingers at each other: John had blamed Tony, and now Tony suggested John was lying to shift the blame. The truth, perhaps, lay somewhere in between, with each man playing a part in Kathleen's fate.

The second Strange murder trial—Commonwealth of Kentucky vs. Anthony Eugene Jones for the murder of Kathleen Strange—began in early 1994. This trial received less attention than John's, partly because much of the gruesome story had already been told and partly because Tony's fate (533 years in prison) was essentially sealed regardless of the outcome. Prosecutors argued that even if John had physically carried out parts of the crime, it was Tony who had the motive and vicious intent to kill his own mother. They proposed a scenario in which Tony, fueled by anger and perhaps seeking money, confronted Kathleen and pulled the trigger, after which John helped cover it up. They highlighted Tony's proven capacity for violence and hate, as evidenced by the Cherokee Park killing.

Tony's defense took the opposite approach from John's. They insisted John alone had killed Kathleen in a domestic quarrel and that John's attempt to blame Tony was a desperate lie. They reminded jurors that a prior jury had convicted John of actually committing the murder, so why revisit those facts? The defense also emphasized that Tony had no forensic ties to the crime scene. No fingerprints, no DNA—though DNA testing was rudimentary at the time—and no eyewitnesses. Essentially, Tony's team argued that the state was trying to convict him based solely on the word of John Strange, a proven murderer, and the coincidence of Tony's later crime.

The truth of Kathleen's murder may never be fully untangled. After days of testimony, the jury in Tony's trial faced a reasonable doubt conundrum. In June 1994, the verdict came: Tony Jones was acquitted of direct involvement in Kathleen Strange's murder. Lacking concrete evidence, jurors were not convinced beyond a reasonable doubt that

Tony had actively participated in killing his mother. Some jurors later said that while Tony's potential involvement was suspicious, the case presented felt largely speculative. In effect, Kathleen's murder remains officially attributed to John Strange alone, who has never wavered from his story blaming Tony.

Nonetheless, Tony did not escape accountability. The legal saga concluded with Tony remaining in prison on his 533-year sentence for the Cherokee Park murder—a punishment that all but ensures he will never be released. John Strange, now in his mid-70s, likewise remains incarcerated, serving out his sixty-five-year term in a Kentucky state penitentiary. According to prison records, John will not be eligible for release until well into his 90s. Both men, once free and part of a family unit, will likely die behind bars.

As for Christine Strange and Sam Edwards, the peripheral accomplices, their fates were far less severe. In exchange for her crucial testimony against her father, Christine received a plea deal on the evidence-tampering charge. She was sentenced to probation and mandatory counseling, avoiding jail time. Sam Edwards also pleaded guilty to tampering and received a short jail sentence, partly suspended. The court acknowledged that Christine and Sam were young and influenced by John, though many still faulted them for not coming forward sooner. Their attempt to wash away the bloodstains—literally and figuratively—will haunt them for life.

The Strange case transfixed the Louisville community in the early 1990s. Media coverage was extensive, with local newspapers following every development from the initial fire to the trials and retrials. Local television news carried somber reports, and anchors spoke of the "decapitation murder" in tones of disbelief. It wasn't just the gore that captured public attention—it was the disturbing notion that a seemingly ordinary family could implode in such a violent, twisted way.

At Kathleen's former school and church, grief was compounded by horror. A memorial service for Kathleen was held in June 1990 once her remains were released for burial. Colleagues and students remembered her as a kind teacher taken too soon. A minister addressing the congregation warned of "the evil that can hide behind a friendly face" in reference to John Strange. Indeed, many who knew John casually—as a teacher, neighbor, or church member—were stunned that he could commit such a crime.

How could a devout Baptist schoolteacher also be a murderer who would mutilate his wife? This jarring contradiction became a talking point in Louisville. It echoed, for some, another notorious Louisville case from just two years prior: the murder of Brenda Schaefer by Mel Ignatow in 1988. Ignatow, like John Strange, had seemed unremarkable outwardly, yet he had committed unspeakable acts. The early 1990s in Louisville were marked by the realization that horrific violence could lurk behind mundane façades.

CHAPTER 6
THE VANISHING

The crisp November air settled over St. Paul, Minnesota, as the sun set on an ordinary Tuesday evening in 1981. Families across the Midway neighborhood hurried through their evening routines, with some heading to work, others to dinner, and many to local community events. Among them, the Hansen family—mother Ellen, six-year-old Cassandra "Cassie," and four-year-old Vanessa—bundled up against the chill and made their way to the Jehovah Evangelical Lutheran Church for a special family night program. The church sat like a steadfast guardian on Snelling Avenue, its warm lights beckoning parishioners inside, away from the darkening November sky.

Inside, the church basement buzzed with activity. Children darted about in excitement, parents chatted, and volunteers organized activities for the evening's festivities. Cassie, a bright, book-loving first grader with blonde hair and an eager smile, stayed close to her mother and sister as they settled in for the children's program. The church auditorium, filled with the comforting sounds of community and fellowship, was typical Tuesday night fare for this close-knit congregation. No one could have imagined that within the safe confines of this sacred space, evil lurked in the shadows, watching and waiting.

What happened next would shatter not only one family's world but also an entire community's sense of security. The events of November 10, 1981, would forever change how parents in St. Paul viewed their children's safety, even in places once considered sanctuaries from the dangers of the outside world. Tragically, this ordinary evening was the last time anyone would see little Cassie Hansen alive.

At approximately 6:50 p.m., as the children's scavenger hunt was about to begin, Cassie tugged at her mother's sleeve and asked for permission to use the bathroom. Ellen Hansen, seeing nothing unusual in this request within the familiar church setting, nodded and watched her daughter skip away. The church had restrooms on both the main floor and upstairs, and while Ellen expected Cassie to use the nearby facilities on the lower level, the little girl apparently decided to head upstairs instead—perhaps to the bathroom she knew better.

Those fleeting moments as Cassie walked away marked the last time her mother would see her daughter alive, a mundane parting with no opportunity for a proper goodbye.

Three witnesses later recalled seeing Cassie in the hallway and stairwell during those critical minutes. They noticed the small blonde girl making her way toward the upper level of the church. More significantly, two of those same witnesses observed something else: an unfamiliar middle-aged man lingering in the same hallway, heading up the same stairs shortly after Cassie went in that direction.

By 7:05 p.m., Ellen Hansen grew concerned. The bathroom trip was taking far too long. Rising from her seat, she went to check the restroom herself but found no sign of her daughter. What followed was a parent's worst nightmare unfolding in real time—the frantic checking of stalls, the quickening pace down hallways, the initial voice of reason saying perhaps Cassie had wandered off to explore. But as minutes stretched on and more people joined the search, a cold dread settled over the church.

Every corner of the building was searched. Cassie's coat remained behind in the auditorium—a small, poignant detail that suggested she hadn't planned to go outside. By 7:30 p.m., with the little girl nowhere to be found, the police were called. Officers Jim Groh and Rick Klein arrived promptly, young men who would later recall that even in those early moments, they sensed something deeply wrong.

Through the night, an agonizing search expanded beyond the church walls. Flashlight beams cut through the darkness as officers and volunteers combed the surrounding streets and alleys. Local television stations broadcast Cassie's photo and description, while taxi drivers and patrol officers across the city were alerted to watch for a small blonde girl, possibly in distress, possibly with a stranger. The community response was immediate and overwhelming, but as midnight came and went with no sign of Cassie, hope began to dim.

What no one realized as they searched was that Cassie was already beyond help. In those brief moments after she left her mother's side, she had encountered a diabolical predator in the stairwell. While desperate searches continued through the night, Cassie's life had already been extinguished and her small body hidden away, waiting to be discarded like refuse.

St. Paul, still reeling from a bizarre kidnapping case just the year before, when Ming Sen Shiue had not only abducted a woman and her daughter but also murdered a six-year-old boy who witnessed the crime, now faced another unthinkable tragedy involving a child. The sense of vulnerability was overwhelming, especially because, this time, the victim had vanished from inside a church—a location where most parents felt their children were safe from the evils of the world.

November 11, 1981, Veterans Day, dawned with the city already awake and searching. Many police officers and volunteers had been up all night looking for any trace of Cassie Hansen. The grim answer to their efforts came shortly before 11:00 a.m., when an employee behind an auto repair shop made a horrifying discovery.

Behind the Auto Clinic Garage at the corner of Grand Avenue and Grotto Street, approximately three miles from the church, the worker approached a large commercial dumpster and found the body of a small child discarded among the trash. Police were summoned immediately, and the worst fears of the community were confirmed: the body was that of Cassie Hansen.

The dumpster and surrounding area became a crime scene, cordoned off with yellow tape as detectives and crime scene technicians meticulously collected evidence. The medical examiner who arrived on the scene determined that Cassie had been killed by ligature strangulation, consistent with a belt being used as a garrote. The time of death was estimated between 8:00 p.m. and midnight the previous evening, just hours after she had disappeared from the church.

The autopsy revealed the brutality of Cassie's final moments. The child had been severely beaten, with bruises and trauma visible on her face, head, ribs, and shoulder. Marks on her face matched the pattern of a hand clamped tightly over her mouth—a stark indication of her terrified struggle as her attacker had silenced her. Though there were no signs of penetrative sexual assault, investigators discovered semen stains on Cassie's clothing, indicating a sexual motive. The killer had likely molested the child and ejaculated on her clothing even without committing rape.

This bodily fluid provided investigators with their first solid forensic lead. Though DNA profiling was still years away from becoming standard procedure, crime lab technicians could perform blood typing on the semen. Analysis showed the perpetrator had Type O blood and was a secretor, meaning his blood type antigens appeared in other bodily fluids. While this couldn't identify a specific individual, it narrowed the suspect pool to roughly thirty-six percent of the male population.

Another crucial piece of evidence came from a single foreign hair recovered from Cassie's clothing. Microscopic analysis revealed rare ring-shaped banding along the hair shaft—an unusual characteristic that experts believed could be distinctive enough to link a future suspect to the crime.

As news of Cassie's murder spread, additional evidence began surfacing in the streets of St. Paul. On the morning of November 11, a man bicycling down Milton Street had spotted a small black patent leather shoe lying in the road. He remembered seeing a car parked on that block the night before, with a man inside who seemed out of place. The cyclist turned the shoe over to police, and Cassie's family confirmed it as one she had worn to church. The matching shoe was discovered the following day in the same area. Investigators noted that both shoes were missing their metal buckles, which appeared to have been forcibly torn off. The scattered footwear, combined with the witness sighting, helped police begin to trace the killer's movements across the city.

The scattered evidence, the body in a dumpster, shoes strewn along residential streets, and signs of a sexual assault. They all painted a picture of a sexually motivated abduction that turned lethal, likely as the perpetrator attempted to silence his victim. For the investigators working the case, including veteran Ramsey County death investigator Don Gorrie, the crime scene and autopsy findings were deeply disturbing. Gorrie, who had a two-year-old daughter of his own, later admitted that the case stuck with him for years afterward. "It was just hard not to carry that case with me," he confessed.

As the police processed the crime scene, the Hansen family received the devastating news that their little girl would never come home. A community already on edge now faced the realization that a dangerous predator walked among them—one who had taken a child from what should have been one of the safest places in the neighborhood. The pressure on investigators to identify and capture the killer intensified with each passing hour.

While the community mourned and parents kept their children closer than ever, St. Paul's sex homicide unit was already following leads that pointed to one man—a fifty-seven-year-old taxi driver named Stuart Willis Knowlton. Even before Cassie's body was found, a tip had reached police about Knowlton from an unlikely source. Janice Rettman, an employee in the Mayor's Office, contacted WCCO-TV crime reporter Caroline Lowe with concerns about Knowlton's possible involvement based on his known behaviors around children. The reporter passed this information to investigators immediately, putting Knowlton on their radar from the earliest hours of the case.

Knowlton was a somewhat familiar figure in St. Paul's Midway neighborhood, known to loiter near places where children gathered. One acquaintance later noted that Knowlton liked to hang around playgrounds and exhibited an unsettling interest in children. His job as a cab driver provided both opportunity and cover for predatory behavior—he had a vehicle readily available and could claim to be working when questioned about his whereabouts.

As investigators dug deeper into Knowlton's activities on the night of November 10, multiple red flags emerged that could not be dismissed as coincidences.

From approximately 5:00 p.m. until 3:00 a.m. the next morning, Knowlton made no radio contact with his taxi dispatchers. He neither responded to calls nor requested fares during that entire period—highly unusual for a driver who typically maintained active communication with dispatch. This extended silence suggested he was engaged in activities he didn't want to document.

Stuart Knowlton

At approximately 7:50 p.m. on November 10, less than an hour after Cassie disappeared, a witness spotted Knowlton inside an Arthur Treacher's fish and chips restaurant located at Grand and Grotto, virtually the same corner where Cassie's body would later be found. The witness noted that Knowlton loitered there for nearly thirty minutes, appearing nervous and out of place. When the witness left, he observed Knowlton standing outside, staring intently at the Auto Clinic Garage across the street—the very location of the dumpster where Cassie would be discarded.

The witness's account placed Knowlton near the eventual dump site during the likely timeframe of the murder. It seemed plausible that Knowlton had Cassie hidden in his taxi at that very moment, perhaps restrained, as he scoped out a location to dispose of her body.

Around 3:00 a.m. on November 11, Knowlton showed up unannounced at the Comfort Massage Studio in St. Paul. Dorothy Noga, an employee at the parlor, encountered him and immediately sensed something was wrong. He was hunched over, breathing heavily, shaking, and speaking rapidly, his entire demeanor frantic and unsteady. Knowlton claimed he had stopped by just to drop off his business card, but his agitated state suggested something far more troubling. At the time, Dorothy hadn't yet heard about Cassie's disappearance, but the encounter disturbed her enough that she would remember it clearly later.

Just after leaving the massage parlor, Knowlton finally broke his radio silence—not to report any sightings of the missing girl, but to claim that a fare had stolen his briefcase containing his trip sheets, the logs that taxi drivers are required to maintain detailing all passengers. The next day, he contacted a former employer at another cab company and asked to buy blank trip sheets, falsely claiming his current employer didn't supply them. These actions strongly suggested Knowlton was attempting to cover his tracks by destroying or fabricating records of his activities that night.

Perhaps most telling was Knowlton's unusual fixation on the case after Cassie's body was found. During his next taxi shift on November 11, he twice broke protocol by using the cab radio to rant about the murder and the ongoing investigation. Each time, the dispatcher had to cut him off, reminding him that such use of the radio was inappropriate. His coworkers found it strange that he seemed so obsessed with this particular crime. Of course, criminals often insert themselves into investigations, driven by guilt or a morbid fascination with their own handiwork.

Given this constellation of suspicious circumstances, the St. Paul police quickly zeroed in on Stuart Knowlton. Police questioned Knowlton on November 12, just one day after Cassie's body was found, but released him due to a lack of physical evidence at the time. Though they didn't yet have enough evidence to arrest him, investigators quietly put him under surveillance as they continued to build their case.

Meanwhile, they sought help from those who knew Knowlton personally, hoping someone might coax out a confession or an incriminating statement. This strategy would lead to one of the most dramatic chapters in the case, involving a brave woman who risked everything to help catch a killer.

Dorothy Noga, a thirty-eight-year-old massage therapist and mother of four, became an unexpected hero in the Cassie Hansen investigation. On the night of November 11, moved by news of the child's murder, Dorothy called the police to report concerns about a different massage client who had made disturbing comments about children. When she spoke to investigators, however, she learned they were already looking at Stuart Knowlton as a suspect—the same man who had visited her studio in an agitated state just hours after Cassie's murder.

In that moment, Dorothy made a critical connection. Knowlton was a regular client who had shared inappropriate sexual fantasies during massage sessions, including scenarios involving children. One fantasy he had described to her bore chilling resemblance to the abduction of a child from a church—the very crime he had apparently just committed. Recognizing she might be in a unique position to help,

Dorothy volunteered to assist the police by contacting Knowlton.

The police were understandably cautious about using a civilian to engage a murder suspect. They initially advised Dorothy not to get involved, as they were concerned for her safety. However, Dorothy was determined. Against police recommendations, she reached out to Knowlton on her own, beginning a dangerous cat-and-mouse interaction that would span several weeks.

On November 17 and 18, 1981, Dorothy made contact with Knowlton by phone. During their conversation on the eighteenth, Knowlton made an astonishing admission: He confessed to killing Cassie Hansen and provided details about the murder that only the perpetrator would know. He described how he had approached the little girl in the church, lured her in with the promise of a game, and then strangled her with his belt when she began screaming. Unfortunately, this crucial confession was not recorded and existed only in Dorothy's memory.

Undeterred, Dorothy continued her dangerous liaison with the killer. On December 8, she met Knowlton in person and drove him past the Jehovah Lutheran Church. When Knowlton realized where they were, he became visibly agitated—a reaction that further convinced Dorothy of his guilt. Five days later, on December 13, they spoke again by phone, and Knowlton once more admitted to the killing. This second confession also went unrecorded due to technical issues.

The situation took a violent turn immediately after this December 13 call. Perhaps sensing that Dorothy posed a threat who could expose him, Knowlton decided to silence her permanently. He showed up at the Comfort Massage

Studio in the early morning hours of December 14, 1981, and Dorothy's coworker let him in, unaware of the danger. Knowlton immediately became aggressive, pushing Dorothy into a chair and putting his face inches from hers.

"Take a look, because it's going to be your last," he snarled, then added ominously, "I'll show you what she went through"—a clear reference to Cassie. With that, Knowlton launched a frenzied knife attack on Dorothy Noga.

The assault was brutal and prolonged. For approximately twenty minutes, Knowlton tried to smother Dorothy and stabbed her thirty-two times. He slashed her throat, severed her carotid artery and jugular vein, and inflicted wounds behind her ear, on her face, and elsewhere on her body. Blood poured from Dorothy like a faucet. As her vision blurred and she began to lose consciousness, she pretended to be dead, praying for help as her life ebbed away.

In what can only be described as divine intervention, help arrived at the critical moment. Officer Pat Scott of the St. Paul Police was on a late-night break at a diner only about 125 feet from the massage parlor when the 911 call came through. He rushed to the scene and found Dorothy Noga collapsed in a pool of blood. Scott immediately grabbed a towel and applied pressure to the most serious neck wound, likely preventing her from bleeding out before paramedics arrived.

Dorothy was rushed to the hospital in critical condition. Doctors later marveled that, "there's absolutely no way in the world that this woman ever should have lived," given the severity of her injuries. The trauma and blood loss from the attack caused Dorothy to suffer memory loss, and she didn't recall Knowlton's confessions until five months later, when her memory gradually returned. Once she recovered, she was able to provide a full statement to the police about Knowlton's admissions.

While Dorothy recovered, investigators continued pursuing other angles. Janice Rettman, who had provided the initial tip, cooperated with police by speaking with Knowlton and secretly recording their conversations. Though he didn't explicitly confess to her, he made incriminating remarks, such as mentioning that Cassie had been strangled—a fact not widely known at the time. He also told Rettman he couldn't remember where he was on the night of the murder and admitted to having an explosive temper.

Another acquaintance, Janice Lloyd, reported that Knowlton had asked her to provide a false alibi for him. Three days after the murder, he called Lloyd and asked if she would say he had phoned her on the night of November 10. Lloyd knew he hadn't called then, and she refused to lie. When she directly asked if he had killed Cassie, he ambiguously replied that he wasn't sure and needed someone to talk to.

By late summer 1982, with Dorothy Noga recovered and able to testify, the case against Stuart Knowlton was ready to proceed. The physical evidence—the semen blood-type match, the distinctive ringed hair comparison that matched Knowlton's, witness sightings placing him at key locations, the shoe trail, and his pattern of suspicious behavior—when combined with Dorothy's testimony about his confessions, created a compelling case. On September 28, 1982, a Ramsey County grand jury indicted Stuart W. Knowlton on three counts of first-degree murder for the death of Cassie Hansen.

By the time Stuart Knowlton faced trial in April 1983, he had suffered his own misfortune. In a strange twist of fate, he had been struck by a vehicle while crossing a street in downtown St. Paul during the investigation, resulting in the amputation of his leg below the knee. This injury did not deter prosecutors, who proceeded with the case against the now-disabled defendant.

In a somewhat surprising legal strategy, Knowlton waived his right to a jury trial, opting instead to be tried by a judge alone. Perhaps his defense believed a judge might be more impartial or better able to sift through potentially prejudicial evidence than a local jury still reeling from the emotional impact of Cassie's murder.

The trial lasted three weeks and presented a wealth of damning evidence. Forensic experts testified about the semen typing that matched Knowlton's blood type, the distinctive banded hair found on Cassie's clothing that matched his, and other physical findings. Witnesses recounted seeing Knowlton at the church and near the dump site on the night of the murder. Taxi dispatchers described his unexplained radio silence during the critical hours, and acquaintances shared his incriminating remarks and behavior in the days following the crime.

Most powerful of all was Dorothy Noga's testimony. Fully recovered but bearing visible scars from Knowlton's attack, she recounted in detail what he had told her about murdering Cassie. She described how he had admitted to entering the church, approaching Cassie with the offer to play a game, leading her to his taxi, and then strangling her with his belt when she began screaming. Dorothy also testified that Knowlton had expressed a sexual fixation on young girls' shoes, specifically ones without buckles, and told her he was disappointed that Cassie's shoes had buckles. She also testified about his subsequent attempt to silence her permanently—a desperate act that further indicated his guilt.

The defense attempted to cast doubt wherever possible, suggesting other leads and pointing out limitations in the forensic evidence. They noted that hair comparison is not absolute proof of identity and emphasized the lack of direct eyewitnesses to the abduction. However, given the mountain of circumstantial evidence and Knowlton's confessions to Dorothy, these arguments gained little traction.

At the conclusion of the trial, the judge found Stuart Knowlton guilty on all three counts of first-degree murder. In June 1983, he was sentenced to life in prison for the first count: murder in the course of criminal sexual conduct. The other two counts were later vacated to avoid redundant convictions.

In Minnesota at that time, a life sentence carried the possibility of parole after serving a minimum term. When Knowlton first became eligible for parole in the late 1990s, the Hansen family mobilized to ensure he would never walk free. For nearly seventeen years after his conviction, they attended parole hearings and submitted emotional pleas to keep him incarcerated. Their advocacy succeeded; he was denied parole repeatedly, thanks in part to Cassie's family, who fought to ensure he remained behind bars.

On October 31, 2006, at the age of seventy-five, Stuart Willis Knowlton died of natural causes while still incarcerated at the Minnesota Correctional Facility – Oak Park Heights. His death came just a couple of weeks before the twenty-fifth anniversary of Cassie's murder, bringing final closure to a case that had haunted St. Paul for a quarter-century.

Cassie Hansen's murder left an indelible mark on St. Paul. In the immediate aftermath, there was a profound shift in how parents viewed their children's safety, even in places once considered sanctuaries. As retired officer Jim Groh recalled, "My kids were scared for years" after Cassie's case, reflecting how even families of police officers changed their habits to protect their children. Another officer noted that life was never the same for children of that era—the freedom to explore independently, to venture into public places without constant supervision, had been severely curtailed by the specter of what happened to one little girl in a church bathroom.

Churches and schools across St. Paul instituted more rigorous supervision policies. Young children were no longer allowed to go to restrooms alone, volunteer hall monitors became standard at events, and parents became hypervigilant about knowing their children's whereabouts at all times. A cousin of Cassie's later admitted that even decades after her murder, he found it impossible to let his own children use public restrooms without supervision—a direct legacy of the trauma that had affected his family.

The case also influenced law enforcement practices in Minnesota. The intensive investigation—involving hundreds of interviews and collaboration with the FBI—became a model for interagency cooperation in child abduction cases. Twenty-three members of the St. Paul Police Department's Sex Crimes Unit received a unit citation for their dedication to solving Cassie's murder.

In 2017, on the thirty-sixth anniversary of Dorothy Noga's near-fatal attack, the department held a ceremony to honor those whose contributions had gone formally unrecognized for decades. Dorothy Noga and Officers Pat Scott, Rick Klein, and Jim Groh received the Chief's Award for Merit. Without Dorothy's bravery, Knowlton might never have been convicted and may have gone on to harm others. At the ceremony, Cassie's surviving sisters, two of whom were born after her death, met and thanked these heroes for the first time. It was a poignant reminder that even though time had passed, Cassie's memory remained alive in the community.

At the Jehovah Evangelical Lutheran Church, a simple plaque was mounted in memory of Cassie Hansen as a subtle yet permanent tribute, ensuring that new generations to pass through those halls would know the history and remain vigilant.

CHAPTER 7
THE NIGHT SHIFT

The unassuming town of Moose Lake, Minnesota, nestled against the shores of its namesake lake, embodied the idyllic peace of rural America. In the late spring of 1999, as the last remnants of winter finally released their grip on the northern landscape, the community of 2,200 residents welcomed the gentler season with a collective sigh of relief. Memorial Day weekend had just passed, and the first hint of summer was settling comfortably across the small lakeside town.

The roads running through Moose Lake served as vital arteries connecting the Twin Cities to the south with Duluth to the north, bringing travelers and truckers alike through the quiet community. Interstate 35 hummed with constant traffic, and alongside it, local businesses thrived, catering to both residents and those just passing through. Among these establishments stood D.J.'s Expressway Conoco station, a combination gas station and convenience store that served as a familiar landmark to locals.

For nineteen-year-old Katie Poirier, the station represented more than just another business—it was her workplace, a stepping stone toward the future she envisioned for herself. Katie was a familiar face to residents of Moose Lake and nearby Barnum, where she had grown up. Standing at just 5'3" with a slight build, Katie's petite frame disguised her considerable determination. Those who knew her described her as a friendly, hard-working young woman who approached life with quiet confidence and an infectious smile.

Katie had graduated from Barnum High School the previous year, a popular student with a wide circle of friends. Unlike many peers who drifted aimlessly after graduation, Katie had clear ambitions. She dreamed of building a career in criminal justice, hoping one day to become a corrections officer. The late-night shifts at D.J.'s Expressway were simply a means to an end—a way to earn money and gain experience while moving toward her goals.

The convenience store job wasn't particularly glamorous, but it suited Katie's needs. Management trusted her implicitly, often leaving her to handle the store alone during overnight hours. In a town like Moose Lake, where serious crime was virtually non-existent, such arrangements weren't considered risky. The community maintained a pervasive sense of safety, neighbors looked out for one another, and strangers were welcomed with typical Midwestern hospitality.

Nothing in Katie's upbringing or daily life would have suggested she might be in danger. Growing up in rural Minnesota had instilled in her a natural trust in others, perhaps even a certain innocence. Like countless other young adults working similar jobs across America's heartland, Katie likely never imagined that a routine shift could escalate into anything sinister.

However, as the mild evening of May 26, 1999, descended on Moose Lake, the security that Katie and her community had long taken for granted was about to be shattered in the most chilling way imaginable.

The evening of Wednesday, May 26, 1999, began unremarkably at D.J.'s Expressway. Katie had arrived for her shift and settled into the familiar routine of stocking shelves, assisting customers, and managing the register. The spring night was pleasant, the temperature was mild, and traffic flowed steadily along the interstate as usual. Nothing distinguished this particular evening from countless others Katie had worked at the convenience store.

As the clock approached midnight, the store had grown quieter. The late-night rush of travelers had dwindled to occasional customers stopping for fuel or coffee to ward off highway drowsiness. Alone in the store, as was typical for that time of night, Katie likely anticipated closing soon. Perhaps she was already thinking about heading home, where she would be expected by her family in neighboring Barnum.

But at precisely 11:40 p.m., the store's security camera captured a moment that would haunt the region for years to come. The grainy black-and-white footage revealed a profoundly disturbing scene: a man in jeans and a backward baseball cap escorting Katie out of the store. He wore a distinctive vintage New York Yankees jersey—number 23—and moved with deliberate purpose. Most chilling was his hand, clearly visible against the back of Katie's neck as he propelled her forward. At one point in the footage, Katie reflexively raised her own hand toward her throat in a gesture investigators would later interpret as evidence that her abductor may have looped some type of cord around her neck to maintain control.

The expressions on their faces weren't clearly visible on the grainy tape, but Katie's body language told its own story. She appeared compliant yet tense, moving under duress rather than by choice. In those few seconds of silent surveillance footage, the young woman's terror was palpable even through the primitive technology of the store's security system.

Minutes later, a customer pulled into the station and immediately sensed something was wrong. The store stood eerily empty, lights still blazing but no clerk in sight. At 12:07 a.m., the concerned patron called the police to report that the station was unattended. Moose Lake officers responded promptly, discovering Katie's personal belongings still in the store but no sign of the young woman herself. Upon reviewing the security tape, they witnessed the terrifying abduction scene unfold on the monitor before them.

The officers could discern enough from the footage to form a basic description of the suspect: A white male of average build, approximately five feet ten inches tall and around 170 pounds, wearing a backward baseball cap and a Yankees jersey. He appeared to have longer, light-colored hair, and his dress and mannerisms suggested he might be in his mid-twenties.

The realization set in quickly—they were dealing with a kidnapping. Calls went out immediately, alerting law enforcement across the region. Katie's family received the news no parent ever wants to hear: Their daughter had vanished, taken by force by an unknown assailant.

The news of Katie's abduction spread through Moose Lake and surrounding towns like wildfire. By dawn on May 27, the normally tranquil community had transformed into a hive of frantic activity. Katie's family, friends, neighbors, and even perfect strangers converged to assist in what would become one of the largest search operations in the region's history.

Hundreds of volunteers reported to hastily established coordination centers, ready to comb every inch of the surrounding countryside. Police K9 units attempted to track Katie's scent while helicopters swept low over the terrain, scanning the dense Minnesota woods and highway corridors of Carlton County for any sign of the missing teenager. Volunteers and officers methodically searched ditches, back roads, and forested areas, calling Katie's name into the silence.

Flyers bearing Katie's photograph and details quickly appeared in shop windows and on highway billboards throughout northeastern Minnesota. Local radio stations interrupted regular programming with descriptions of Katie and her abductor, imploring listeners to call with information, no matter how seemingly insignificant. The community's response was immediate and overwhelming—a testament to the tight-knit nature of rural Minnesota and the collective horror felt at the brazen kidnapping of one of their own.

Meanwhile, investigators from the Carlton County Sheriff's Office and the Minnesota Bureau of Criminal Apprehension (BCA) worked around the clock, interviewing employees of nearby businesses and potential witnesses who had been near the gas station that night. Several bystanders reported seeing a black pickup truck lingering suspiciously in the vicinity of D.J.'s Expressway around the time of the abduction. One woman mentioned that the male driver had been loitering outside the Subway sandwich shop located in the same building, and his presence had made her uneasy. Crucially, at least one witness managed to recall a partial license plate from the suspicious vehicle—three numbers and a letter that would later prove vital to the investigation.

Within the first twenty-four hours, law enforcement released a composite sketch based on descriptions from four witnesses. The image depicted a young Caucasian man with light, shaggy hair and average features. This sketch, along with stills from the surveillance video and the vehicle description, was distributed to news outlets across the state. The case rapidly gained prominence in Minnesota, dominating headlines and newscasts as the public's fear and fascination grew in equal measure.

The abduction struck a nerve precisely because it undermined fundamental assumptions about safety in small-town America. The idea that a young woman could be forcibly taken from a well-lit, public place sent ripples of anxiety through communities across the region. Parents kept children closer, women avoided working alone at night, and a general unease settled over areas that had previously felt immune to such dangers.

Tips began flooding police hotlines, with over 3,500 leads eventually logged during the investigation. The FBI joined the case due to the possibility of interstate kidnapping, bringing in additional resources and expertise. Investigators checked on registered sex offenders in the region and contacted a nearby facility that housed sex offenders to confirm all inmates were accounted for. This initial sweep failed to produce obvious suspects, forcing authorities to cast a wider net and pursue creative investigative strategies.

In an unconventional twist, investigators sought help from NASA's Jet Propulsion Laboratory to enhance the surveillance footage. Using technology typically reserved for space imaging, NASA specialists worked to clarify the grainy video frames. While this high-tech effort couldn't produce a crystal-clear identification, it helped confirm certain details about the suspect's appearance, including details about the Yankees jersey.

As days stretched into weeks with no sign of Katie, hope mingled with dread. Her mother expressed a gut feeling that Katie might still be found safe, which kept volunteers motivated during the exhausting search efforts. Law enforcement, however, grew increasingly concerned that, with each passing day, the likelihood of finding Katie alive diminished significantly.

To maintain public interest and generate new leads, investigators made a unique appeal. Believing the suspect might be a baseball fan based on his Yankees jersey, they enlisted Minnesota Twins legend Paul Molitor to make a televised plea for information. Molitor's appeal, broadcast about two weeks into the search, reached viewers across the state—including one man whose suspicions would finally break the case wide open.

On June 18, 1999, a man named Darrel Brown contacted the tip line with information that would dramatically alter the course of the investigation. Brown, an employee at the

Minnesota Veterans Home in Minneapolis, had been watching coverage of the case when something had clicked in his mind. He informed investigators that the man in the composite sketch strongly resembled a former co-worker named Donald "Don" Hutchinson, a janitor who had recently quit his job without explanation.

Brown's tip was specific and compelling. He noted that Hutchinson drove a black pickup truck that he had suddenly stopped using right after the abduction. Hutchinson had also cut his long, light-brown hair short around that same time and, most suspiciously, had failed to show up for work on May 27—the morning after Katie disappeared. Shortly thereafter, he abruptly quit his position at the Veterans Home. The timing of these actions, all occurring in the immediate aftermath of the crime, had struck Brown as too suspicious to ignore.

Investigators acted quickly, running the name "Donald Hutchinson" through their databases. Initial checks revealed no significant criminal record under that name. However, when they checked vehicle records, they discovered something crucial—Hutchinson's registered pickup truck had a license plate beginning with the very characters witnesses had recalled from the scene.

As police dug deeper, they uncovered something even more alarming: "Donald Hutchinson" was actually an alias. The man's real name was Donald Albin Blom, a registered sex offender who had a history of abducting petite, young girls just like Katie. Blom had apparently deceived his employer by using a false surname; the supervisors at the Veterans Home had been unaware of his criminal past.

Donald Blom

When investigators uncovered Blom's true identity, his violent history came into sharp focus. The fifty-year-old had multiple convictions for kidnapping and sexual assault, with a disturbing pattern of targeting young women. A quick review of his prior cases revealed that he had previously abducted victims with profiles similar to Katie—petite, young females. The investigation had finally found its prime suspect.

Authorities surveilled Blom's residence in Richfield, near Minneapolis, but discovered he wasn't home. They soon learned that Blom, under his Hutchinson alias, owned a twenty-acre rural property near Moose Lake, only about twelve miles from where Katie was abducted. This geographic connection added another compelling layer to the mounting evidence.

Neighbors near that property told police that Blom had spent considerable time there before late May, often camping or fishing on the land. However, they hadn't seen him there at all in the weeks since Katie's disappearance. It seemed that after the night of May 26, Blom had deliberately avoided returning to his Moose Lake acreage, even allowing the grass to grow tall and his chores to lapse—behavior they considered out of character for him.

With probable cause accumulating rapidly, law enforcement obtained search warrants for Blom's house, vehicles, and land. A task force was assembled to locate and apprehend him before he could potentially flee or harm anyone else.

On June 22, 1999, a team of agents from the Minnesota BCA and local sheriff's office tracked Donald Blom to a campground near Alexandria, Minnesota, about 140 miles from his Richfield home. Blom was staying there with his wife, Amy, and their children, apparently trying to maintain a semblance of normal family life even as the manhunt closed in. In the early morning hours, officers approached Blom at the campground, initially engaging him in casual conversation to avoid escalating the situation and potentially provoking panic. Blom quickly realized the purpose of their visit. He was polite and cooperative, neither resisting nor attempting to flee, but he immediately invoked his right to silence, declining to answer questions and requesting an attorney.

Later that day, as Blom and his family were driving back toward the Twin Cities, law enforcement moved in and formally arrested him on suspicion of kidnapping Katie Poirier. When officers got their first close look at the suspect, they noted that his formerly shoulder-length hair had indeed been cut much shorter, consistent with Darrel Brown's tip. He also appeared to have dyed out the blond highlights that witnesses had observed. Despite these alterations to his appearance, at least one eyewitness was able to identify him in a lineup.

Blom was booked and held in the Carlton County Jail while searches of his property commenced. However, he demonstrated his potential for cunning and dangerous behavior almost immediately. Within days of his detention, jail staff discovered evidence of an escape plan Blom was formulating. Maps and notes suggesting a possible jailbreak route were found in his cell, prompting authorities to place him in solitary confinement to prevent any escape attempt.

Meanwhile, Amy Blom initially provided her husband with an alibi, claiming he had been home with her the night of May 26. She claimed that Blom had returned home around 9:30 p.m., they had gone to bed together, and when she awoke the next morning, he was there making coffee, implying he could not have snuck away to commit the crime. Amy added that when she heard about Katie's disappearance on the news, she assumed he would be a suspect given his history of abducting girls, which was why she had paid attention to his whereabouts that night.

With Blom in custody, attention turned to his twenty-acre Moose Lake property. On June 30, law enforcement and volunteers conducted an exhaustive search of the land, which included a mix of meadow and woodland with an old trailer home and various outbuildings. Over 100 National Guard members were deployed to assist, alongside hundreds of civilian volunteers who had been steadfastly looking for Katie for weeks.

The first day of searching yielded little, but a critical discovery was made on July 1, the second day of the search. In a shallow fire pit behind Blom's trailer, searchers noticed fragments mixed in with the ashes that looked suspiciously like bone. Among the charred debris, they also found a small object that resembled part of a human tooth. The fragments were carefully collected and sent to forensic labs for analysis. Initial tests confirmed that the pieces were human bone fragments, although they were extremely burned and broken. The larger object was determined to be a portion of a human tooth, also badly burned.

Given the state of the remains, obtaining DNA was unlikely. Any genetic material in the tooth pulp was probably destroyed by the fire's heat. However, forensic odontologist Dr. Ann Norrlander found traces of dental filling material still clinging to the tooth fragment. By analyzing the chemical composition of the filling's residue, she identified it as a very specific type of amalgam—one that had been recently introduced in dentistry and was not used by all dentists.

Investigators checked Katie's dental records and learned that she had received a filling at her dentist's office in Esko, Minnesota, just weeks before her abduction. The dentist had used the same new 3M brand dental amalgam found on the recovered tooth. Additionally, experts identified the fragment as a lower molar from a young female, consistent with Katie's age and dental history. This forensic linkage provided investigators with the grim confirmation they had dreaded: They had found evidence of Katie's fate.

The search of Blom's land also turned up other incriminating items, such as illegal firearms and pieces of wire that might have been used as a ligature. As a felon, Blom was prohibited from possessing guns. By late July 1999, authorities felt they had enough evidence to formally charge Donald Blom with kidnapping and murder, even though Katie's body was mostly unrecovered.

In an unexpected turn of events on September 8, 1999, Donald Blom agreed to give a full confession to authorities. Up until that point, he had maintained his silence, but now he claimed he wanted to put the matter behind him. Negotiations were made: In exchange for Blom's truthful account of what happened to Katie, prosecutors agreed not to seek the death penalty and to have him serve his time in a prison near his family. With multiple attorneys present to witness that he was acting voluntarily, Blom gave a tearful, 150-minute taped confession.

In his confession, Blom calmly recounted the events of the night of May 26, 1999. He claimed that earlier that day, he had gone fishing at his Moose Lake property before driving back home to Richfield. Later that night, restless, he drove back north toward Moose Lake. Along the way, he stopped at a bar for a drink and bought some liquor to go. He said he arrived at D.J.'s Expressway convenience store around closing time and saw Katie cleaning up inside.

According to Blom, he didn't know Katie at all—she was a random victim. He described entering the store and, on a sudden impulse, making a grab for her. Katie reacted by bolting toward the door and running outside, but Blom caught up to her in the parking lot. He forced her into his black pickup truck and restrained her. Blom claimed that Katie pleaded with him several times during the drive, asking him to let her go, but she didn't physically resist much until later.

Blom told investigators that he took Katie to his trailer on his rural Moose Lake land. There, in the darkness of the early morning hours, he said he was overcome with a mixture of guilt, panic, and feeling "stupid." As Katie begged for her life, Blom said something in him snapped. He came up behind her and wrapped his hands around her throat. "Then I choked her and killed her," he admitted on tape. He described strangling Katie from behind and said that it took approximately twenty minutes of sustained pressure before she stopped moving.

After ensuring Katie was dead, Blom set about disposing of the evidence. He carried her lifeless body out to the fire pit behind the trailer. He placed her in the pit in a fetal position, piled wood and paper on top of her, and ignited the fire. He fed the flames continuously, attempting to cremate her remains using the makeshift bonfire. By the time he was done, he believed the body had been reduced to ash and a few bone fragments. He scattered what he could and left the site.

Some aspects of Blom's confession contradicted the evidence or witness accounts. For example, he insisted that after grabbing Katie, he simply walked her out of the store with a hand on her arm or shoulder, whereas the surveillance tape clearly showed him gripping the back of her neck and likely using a ligature. He also claimed Katie only fought back once they reached his property, not at the store, which seemed at odds with her evident attempt to flee initially. Moreover, his claim of using just wood and paper to incinerate a body struck investigators as dubious; typically, such a fire would not reach temperatures high enough to cremate remains so completely.

Despite these inconsistencies, the core of his confession aligned with the evidence: He had abducted, killed, and burned Katie Poirier. After giving his statement, Blom even took the unusual step of personally calling two local television stations from jail to announce that he had confessed, wanting the media to know that he'd done what they were asking and to leave his family alone.

For Katie's family, who had held out hope that she might be alive somewhere through five agonizing weeks, the confession was devastating. They learned that Katie had cruelly lost her life on the same night she was taken, and her body had been desecrated.

Yet, even with a full confession on record, the legal journey was far from over. Not long after his dramatic admission, Donald Blom changed his story once again. He told his attorneys that the confession he gave was false—a product of psychological pressure rather than truth. Blom claimed that weeks of solitary confinement in jail, combined with being on ten different medications, had caused him to hallucinate and believe that confessing was the only way out of his oppressive situation. In Blom's new version of events, he had just told authorities what they wanted to hear to escape the stress of his cell. This about-face meant that any plea deal was off, and prosecutors prepared to take the case to trial.

Donald Blom's murder trial began in June 2000, a little over a year after Katie's disappearance. Due to intense publicity surrounding the case, the proceedings were moved from Carlton County to St. Louis County on Minnesota's Iron Range. Even with the change of venue, finding impartial jurors proved challenging, with jury selection alone taking five weeks.

What followed was approximately five more weeks of testimony in a courtroom packed with spectators and media. The prosecution methodically laid out a comprehensive case against Blom, while the defense attempted to cast doubt on the evidence and highlight inconsistencies.

The prosecution opened by walking the jury through the night of the crime and the subsequent investigation. The surveillance video of the abduction was played for the courtroom, creating a hushed atmosphere as jurors watched the grainy images of Katie being led away by a man in a Yankees jersey. Some of the most damning testimony came from a select few witnesses who provided crucial pieces to the puzzle.

Blom's own brother took the stand and testified that he had once given a box of old clothing to the Blom family, including a New York Yankees jersey with the number 23 on it. This directly contradicted Blom's prior claim to police that he had never owned a Yankees jersey and placed the distinctive shirt in his possession.

In a bold move, the prosecution called two women whom Blom had kidnapped in 1983, when they were teenagers, to testify about their ordeal. Normally, prior bad acts are inadmissible, but the judge allowed this testimony to show a pattern, given the striking similarities. The women recounted how Blom abducted them, tied them to a tree, threatened them with a knife, stuffed socks in their mouths, and repeatedly choked one of them unconscious, only to revive her and continue the torture. These harrowing accounts undoubtedly made a strong impression on the jury, illustrating Blom's capacity for violence.

Forensic odontologist Dr. Ann Norrlander testified about her examination of the burned tooth fragment found in Blom's fire pit. She explained how she ultimately identified it as a human tooth with a distinctive filling material. Dr. Norrlander candidly admitted that, at first, she wasn't even sure it was a tooth and that forensic odontology can be "more art than science" in some respects. However, with the aid of Katie's dental records and the chemical analysis of the filling, she was able to conclude "to a reasonable degree of dental certainty" that the tooth belonged to Katie Poirier.

Perhaps the most powerful piece of evidence was Blom's own confession tape, which the judge had allowed despite the defense's objections. The jury was given transcripts and listened to Blom speak in his own words about kidnapping and killing Katie. Hearing the defendant calmly describe the murder had a palpable effect in the courtroom. The Poirier family quietly sobbed as the tape played, and even jurors appeared shaken.

The defense, led by attorney Rodney Brodin, faced an uphill battle. With Blom's confession in evidence and even his spouse initially alibiing him, Brodin needed to create reasonable doubt wherever possible. The defense focused on challenging the reliability of identification and forensic evidence, presenting an alibi, and suggesting an alternate suspect.

Amy Blom took the stand and testified that Blom was at home with her on the night of May 26—coming home around 9:30 p.m., going to bed together, and him being there when she woke up. She explained she paid attention to that night because the news of a Moose Lake abduction caught her attention the next day, and knowing of her husband's past, she thought he might be suspected. Amy also accused the police of coercive interrogation tactics, claiming officers yelled at her, called her a liar, and threatened to take away her children if she didn't say what they wanted.

Challenging the identifications, the defense highlighted that out of six key witnesses who had seen the suspect or the truck, only one had identified Blom with certainty from a lineup. The others were unsure or chose different people. The composite sketch, while similar, was not a perfect likeness of Blom either.

In a somewhat risky move, Donald Blom himself took the stand in his own defense. By testifying, he opened himself up to cross-examination, but he likely felt he had to personally refute his confession in front of the jury. On the stand, Blom flatly denied kidnapping or killing Katie Poirier. He acknowledged making a confession earlier, but he also asserted it was a stupid mistake and false. He claimed he confessed out of desperation to get out of solitary confinement and protect his family from media harassment. Blom grew emotional on the stand, alternating between calmly giving answers and breaking down in tears, portraying himself as a victim of false accusations.

During cross-examination, the prosecution methodically went through Blom's confession point by point. When asked why he gave so many detailed facts if it was all made up, Blom mostly replied with terse yes or no answers, refusing to elaborate. At one point, Blom grew visibly irritated and even told the prosecutor he was getting upset with the questioning. The cross-examination highlighted inconsistencies and lies Blom had told during the investigation, which likely hurt his credibility with the jury.

After closing arguments, in which the prosecution asserted that all evidence pointed irrefutably to Blom and the defense warned of convicting an innocent man based on a coerced confession, the case went to the jury. The jury of twelve men and women began deliberations on August 16, 2000. Given the volume of evidence, they took their time—in total, deliberations lasted ten hours spread over two days, including about three hours spent reviewing the confession tapes again in the jury room.

On August 18, 2000, the jury returned with a verdict. They found Donald Albin Blom guilty on all counts, including first-degree murder while committing kidnapping and first-degree kidnapping. The verdict was unanimous. Jurors later indicated that the forensic evidence and Blom's own words were most convincing, and the defense's alternative theories simply didn't hold water in the face of everything. Blom himself showed little emotion as the verdict was read, though he reportedly turned and told his family that he hadn't killed Katie Poirier, even as he was led away.

Because Blom was convicted of first-degree murder in the course of kidnapping, Minnesota law mandated a sentence of life in prison without the possibility of parole under the state's Paul Antonich Law. On August 22, 2000, the judge formally imposed a life term on Blom. Additionally, for the separate charge of being a felon in possession of a firearm stemming from the guns found on his property, Blom received a nineteen-year prison sentence.

For Katie Poirier's family, the verdict provided some measure of justice but not full closure. Her father, Steve Poirier, told the media that it was "another step to closure.

It'll probably never be closed, but it's a giant step." The knowledge that Blom would never walk free was a relief, but the loss of Katie—and the fact that her body was never recovered for a proper burial—remained an open wound.

The abduction and murder of Katie Poirier had a profound impact on her community and the state of Minnesota. The crime shattered the sense of security that had long prevailed in Moose Lake and similar small towns. Gas station owners in the region began reconsidering late-night staffing policies, and many implemented a two-clerk rule at night or installed improved security systems in the wake of Katie's case.

Perhaps the most significant legacy of this case is the reforms it spurred in Minnesota's laws regarding violent and sexual offenders. Outrage over how Blom, with five sex offense convictions, could be free to commit such a crime led to swift legislative action. In the year following the trial, Minnesota lawmakers crafted a package of measures collectively referred to as "Katie's Law." These measures, passed in 2000, aimed to tighten the supervision of repeat offenders and close the loopholes Blom had exploited.

Key components of Katie's Law included improved criminal information sharing, allowing different jurisdictions, such as police, courts, and corrections, to more readily share data on offenders. The law also strengthened predatory offender registration requirements, with more frequent address verification checks and increased penalties for failing to update one's information. Additionally, the legislation made it more difficult for felons—especially sex offenders—to change their names, addressing how Blom had used name changes to conceal his identity.

Despite maintaining his innocence, Donald Blom was transferred to a federal prison facility in Waynesburg,

Pennsylvania, to serve his life term. He spent years filing unsuccessful appeals, with his final rejection by the Minnesota Supreme Court coming in December 2007. In prison, Blom remained a manipulative figure. In 2006, he tantalized investigators with an offer to confess to other unsolved crimes if authorities would transfer him to a facility closer to his family in Minnesota. However, after leading detectives on for three days without giving any real confession, he backed out of the arrangement.

On January 10, 2023, Donald Blom died in custody at the age of seventy-three. Prison officials reported that Blom had been suffering from significant health issues, and his death was due to natural causes. He died having served about twenty-three years of his life term, all the while maintaining his innocence.

CHAPTER 8
THE KILLER POET

On a crisp March morning in 2005, two plainclothes Illinois state troopers entered the Third Unitarian Church in Chicago's Austin neighborhood. They approached the church secretary with a ruse, showing her a photograph of a man they claimed to be looking for. As they spoke, a gray-haired, bearded man in his mid-60s walked into the office to pick up a business card. The officers immediately recognized him from a photo they had seen, and they casually asked his name.

"J.J. Jameson," he replied, adding a comment about how bad crime was in the neighborhood.

The officers moved in and placed him under arrest. For a split second, the man appeared shocked—the mask of J.J. Jameson shattered instantly. However, he quickly regained his composure. As they walked him out of the church in handcuffs, he sighed and said resignedly, "Well, I've had a good twenty years."

J.J. Jameson wasn't his real name. He was Norman Porter Jr., a convicted double murderer who had escaped from a

Massachusetts prison twenty years earlier. Since his escape, he had completely reinvented himself as a respected poet, church historian, and beloved community figure in Chicago. Now, his double life was suddenly over.

Norman Arthur Porter Jr. was born on January 28, 1940, in Woburn, Massachusetts, as one of four children in a strict New England household. His father ran a well-drilling and house-moving business and instilled a strong work ethic in his children from a young age. Despite this upbringing, Porter began getting into trouble in adolescence. By age thirteen, he had started down a delinquent path, and at fifteen, he was arrested for stealing a car.

That car theft landed the teenage Porter in Lyman School for Boys, a reform school notorious for its harsh conditions. Porter later claimed the experience brutalized him. He emerged traumatized and rebellious, frequently escaping from the institution. Porter claimed he "busted out of Lyman about eighteen times," often stealing cars and joyriding until recapture. On one teenage escapade, he made it as far as Richmond, Virginia, before being caught. This pattern of escape and recapture foreshadowed the dramatic turns his adult life would take.

By age twenty in 1960, Porter was out of reform school but already an experienced petty criminal. He fell in with two other young Boston-area thieves, Theodore "Teddy" Mavor and John Deveau. Together, they embarked on a minor crime spree in the fall of 1960. Porter was actually out on bail for three pending felony charges when the trio set their sights on a clothing retailer in Saugus that night—a decision that would turn deadly.

On the night of September 29, 1960, Porter and Mavor entered the Robert Hall clothing store in Saugus, Massachusetts, a working-class suburb north of Boston. Both men wore blue-and-white bandannas over their faces and low-pulled hats as disguises. They expected to find only a few employees closing up for the night, but the store had stayed open late for the back-to-school shopping rush. Inside were twenty to thirty customers and staff.

Brandishing firearms, the two men herded the shoppers and employees into a back room at gunpoint. Mavor, who had worked briefly at that store months prior, carried a pistol and took charge of the store manager, forcing him toward the office to open the safe. Porter was armed with a sawed-off shotgun and had a revolver tucked in his belt. While Mavor dealt with the manager and the safe, Porter moved through the frightened crowd, demanding wallets and valuables.

One of the store clerks corralled in that back room was twenty-two-year-old John "Jackie" Pigott, who was working a part-time evening shift. Pigott was known as a friendly, hardworking young man who dug ditches by day for the gas company. Confronted by Porter's shotgun, Pigott fumbled to comply with the robber's orders. Porter thrust a raincoat at Pigott and barked, "Put your wallet in this." Pigott nervously replied that he didn't carry a wallet. "Well, put your money in it, then," Porter growled. Pigott managed to pull out two ten-dollar bills, but in his trembling state, he had difficulty sliding the cash into the raincoat pocket. A woman next to him tried to steady the coat to help. At that moment, Pigott inexplicably turned away from Porter—perhaps a reflex or a misunderstanding. Instantly, Porter raised the shotgun and blew a blast into Pigott's neck at point-blank range, killing the young clerk on the spot.

The surrounding hostages screamed and recoiled in horror. Porter coolly bent down, plucked the two ten-dollar bills from Pigott's lifeless hand, and declared, "Now you know I mean business." The robbers continued collecting cash from the others, but chaos was already unfolding: One employee grabbed a stepladder and swung it at Mavor, striking him in the head. The blow knocked Mavor into the store manager, Ralph Fabiano, and the two men scuffled. Mavor's handgun discharged during the struggle, hitting Manager Fabiano in the side. Fortunately, Fabiano survived his wound. The botched robbery was quickly falling apart.

Panicked, Mavor and Porter fled the store with only about $411. Outside, their getaway driver, John Deveau, had apparently lost his nerve; Deveau had heard the gunfire and sped off without them. Porter and Mavor escaped on foot into the night.

The senseless killing of John Pigott devastated his family. His fiancée, nineteen-year-old Claire Wilcox, later recalled that Porter's actions didn't just kill her boyfriend—they "altered the paths of many lives." In the words of Pigott's older brother Robert, "Our parents didn't live a day without my brother's memory. They were denied good things in life after he was taken from them."

After the Saugus robbery, Porter and Mavor were soon captured and charged with first-degree murder. While awaiting trial, Porter was held at the Middlesex County Jail in Cambridge, where security was remarkably lax. It was there, on Mother's Day 1961, that Porter made a daring bid for freedom that turned deadly.

On May 14, 1961, twenty-one-year-old Porter was being escorted back from a visit with a prison psychiatrist when he launched his escape plan. Somehow, Porter had managed to obtain a pistol—likely given to him by an accomplice through the jail's window or visiting area. As he walked down a corridor with an unarmed guard, Porter suddenly pulled out the gun and threatened the guard. He then headed to a nearby room where another inmate, Edgar Cook, was meeting with his attorney. Cook was a high-profile prisoner himself, awaiting trial for murdering a Boston police officer. Brandishing the pistol, Porter waved Cook out of the lawyer conference room, and together, the two inmates rushed for an exit.

Just before they could reach the jail's outer door, they encountered Jail Master David S. Robinson, the fifty-three-year-old head keeper of the facility. Robinson wasn't even supposed to be on duty that day; he had traded shifts so a subordinate could spend Mother's Day with his family. Now Robinson stood in the doorway, blocking the escape path of Porter and Cook. He didn't back down. The jail master ordered Porter to hand over the gun and tried to stall the escape.

Cook urged Porter to shoot Robinson, but Porter hesitated. In that split second, Robinson lunged, attempting to grab Porter and disarm him. A struggle ensued. Porter faltered, Cook snatched the gun from Porter's hand, and he fired at Robinson, shooting the jail master behind the ear at close range. Robinson fell, mortally wounded.

Porter and Cook fled the jail amid the chaos. They split up, and a massive manhunt followed. Cook was found three days later and died in a shootout with police. Porter managed to remain on the lam a bit longer. One week after the jailbreak, he turned up in New Hampshire—where, incredibly, he attempted another armed robbery of a food store. New Hampshire state troopers caught him in the act. At his arraignment, a newspaper photographed Porter smiling, his arms folded confidently, chatting with the arresting troopers as if he hadn't a care in the world.

Back in custody, Porter faced justice for both killings. In 1962, he pleaded guilty to second-degree murder in both cases (Pigott and Robinson). He received a life sentence for each killing, and the judge ordered the sentences to run consecutively, one after the other. As Porter's attorney grimly explained, "You serve life for Robinson's murder, then you die, and then you start serving life for Pigott's murder."

At age twenty-two, Norman Porter began serving what amounted to a double life term in Massachusetts prisons.

Porter's entry into prison coincided with a burgeoning era of prison reform in Massachusetts. In the 1960s and early 1970s, emphasis was placed on the rehabilitation and education of inmates. Porter proved to be an unusually motivated and capable beneficiary of these opportunities.

He earned his high school diploma while incarcerated and pursued college-level courses through Boston University's prison extension program. Under the mentorship of Professor Elizabeth "Ma" Barker—a noted prisoners' rights advocate who taught poetry classes in prison—Porter began exploring literature and creative writing. He discovered a talent for poetry and developed an intellectually curious persona that starkly contrasted with his earlier life as a thug.

Porter founded a prison newspaper and launched a radio program called Radio Free Norfolk, broadcasting from MCI-Norfolk over a local public radio station. The weekly half-hour show earned a 1973 United Press International Citation for Excellence in Public Service. Porter became something of a celebrity inmate, held up as proof that even a convicted murderer could be rehabilitated through education and responsibility.

His transformation into a model inmate earned him increasing privileges. He became a prison trusty and was gradually moved to lower-security facilities. By the 1970s, he had earned enough trust to receive furloughs. On furlough days, he worked as a prison system carpenter and even gave public lectures at churches and colleges about prison reform and poetry.

In 1975, after Porter had served roughly fourteen years, the Massachusetts Advisory Board of Pardons recommended commuting one of his life sentences. The focus was on the David Robinson case. Evidence had emerged indicating that Edgar Cook was the one who had actually shot Jail Master Robinson, not Porter. Combined with Porter's exemplary prison record, there was a compelling argument that at least the Robinson life term could be reduced.

Governor Michael Dukakis accepted the recommendation. On September 3, 1975, Governor Dukakis commuted Porter's life sentence for the murder of David Robinson. The sentence was reduced to thirty-six years and six months, with credit for time served, making Porter immediately eligible for parole on that count. In essence, Porter would now only have to serve out the life sentence for Pigott's murder.

The commutation was not widely publicized—notably, the Robinson family was not even notified that the man convicted of killing their patriarch had received clemency. Flush with this success, Porter turned his hopes to getting his remaining life sentence commuted as well. In 1978, he formally petitioned for a second commutation.

By then, however, the political climate was shifting. When Jackie Pigott's family learned of Porter's bid for clemency, they were outraged. Pigott's cousin, Dorothy "Dottie" Johnson, rallied opposition. Johnson obtained 5,000 signatures from Massachusetts law enforcement officers on a petition demanding no mercy for Porter. Under intense public pressure, the Governor's Council rejected Porter's second commutation request, effectively halting his path to release.

Porter took the failure of his 1978 commutation attempt hard. In April 1980, he simply walked off the grounds of a minimum-security prison—essentially an escape, though a short-lived one. Two days later, Porter returned and turned himself in, claiming that he had wandered away aimlessly due to depression. Because he surrendered so promptly, officials did not prosecute him for this escape.

By the mid-1980s, it became clear to Porter that no further commutations or clemency would be coming his way. Facing the prospect of growing old and dying in prison, Porter made a fateful decision: He would risk everything on one last escape.

On December 23, 1985, Norman Porter carried out one of the simplest yet most brazen prison escapes in Massachusetts history. At the time, forty-five-year-old Porter was being held at the Norfolk Pre-Release Center—essentially a halfway house on the prison grounds where trusted inmates were allowed a degree of freedom. It was an unfenced, minimum-security facility, and inmates could even sign themselves out for short periods. On that day, Porter signed the log to go out on a temporary furlough "walk" and simply never returned.

Porter's escape was clearly premeditated. Minutes before walking away, he was seen making a phone call from a prison payphone. Investigators suspect he had arranged assistance on the outside. According to Porter, he had stashed about $3,000 in cash in plastic bags in the woods near the prison—allegedly money saved from prison labor and speaking fees. After leaving the facility, he claimed he had dug up his hidden cash and caught a bus to Rhode Island. However, law enforcement believed he likely had an accomplice drive him to a distant bus or train station.

One of Porter's long-time mentors, Boston College Professor Robert Castagnola, made no secret of his support. After Porter's disappearance, Castagnola wrote a letter to a Boston newspaper stating, "I fully support Porter's escape... I will be pleased if there is anything I can do to keep Porter out of the clutches of justice and to at last be free." This shocking public endorsement highlighted how deeply some in the community believed in Porter's redemption.

By Christmas 1985, Norman Porter had virtually disappeared. It was an embarrassment for Massachusetts corrections—an inmate convicted of two murders had simply walked out. A fugitive warrant was issued, and manhunts were quietly launched, but there were few initial leads. Porter would later quip that the 1985 escape was his twenty-first successful escape, counting everything from reform school onward.

Norman Porter surfaced in Chicago a short time after his escape, arriving just before New Year's Day 1986. He was drawn to Chicago after reading Nelson Algren's Chicago: City on the Make, which paints Chicago as a haven for hustlers and underworld characters. Upon arrival, Porter checked into a flophouse hotel. Needing a new identity, he thumbed through a telephone directory and plucked a name at random. Norman Porter thus became Jacob "J.J." Jameson.

Norman Porter Jr. (J.J. Jameson)

The next few years were rough and itinerant. Jameson drifted around Chicago, grappling with alcoholism and sometimes living on the streets. He found work as a curbside newspaper vendor, standing at an on-ramp to the Eisenhower Expressway and hawking copies of local newspapers to commuters. By his account, he could make about $50 by 8:30 a.m. doing this before spending his days drinking.

Despite these struggles, Porter formed connections. David Beaton, a progressive-minded local, hired Jameson around 1986 to help renovate a building and let him crash there as a live-in handyman. They struck up a friendship, though Beaton observed that Jameson was "unpredictable and unreliable" when drinking. Beaton had no idea Jameson was a wanted killer. "I never got the sense that he was hiding something," Beaton said later. Jameson told Beaton he was from Maine and had a troubled family background, which explained his lack of ties.

A turning point came around 1988, when Porter wandered into the Third Unitarian Church in the Austin area of Chicago. The church was known for being a social-justice-oriented congregation that welcomed outcasts. Reverend Don Wheat recalled Jameson first showing up with literal "rags around his feet," looking destitute. Reverend Wheat and his church congregants took Jameson under their wing. A church member who owned property hired J.J. as a handyman and provided housing, an arrangement that would repeat many times over the next two decades. The church offered Jameson stability and a sense of belonging that he hadn't had since his prison days.

In Chicago, J.J. Jameson reinvented himself most visibly as a poet. By the early 1990s, he became a familiar face in the city's thriving spoken-word scene. He was in his fifties—decades older than many of the up-and-coming slam poets—but Jameson's colorful personality made him stand out. He cut a memorable figure with his grouchy-yet-humorous stage presence and eccentric outfits, often wearing a bow tie and suspenders to readings. John Starrs, who hosted readings at a local coffee shop, recalled that J.J. had "a whole persona. He would pretend to be gruff... Everybody loved him."

Jameson became a regular at open mic nights across the city. He often served as an emcee or heckler, known for barking "Read the poem!" at any poet who spent too long rambling in their intro. His poetry was described as ironic, humorous, and salty. Over the years, he honed a reputation as a kind of elder statesman of the Chicago poetry circuit—a man seemingly down-and-out yet scholarly and passionate about art.

By 1999, Jameson's work was deemed worthy of publication. A small local press published his chapbook *Lady Rutherford's Cauliflower.* Within the Third Unitarian Church, Jameson rose to be a respected member. He took on the role of church historian and regularly gave lectures or even sermons at the pulpit. J.J. was considered so trustworthy that church friends would give him the keys to their houses and cars.

Jameson had one close call with the law during his time in Chicago. In 1993, he was arrested on minor theft charges under his alias, and his fingerprints were taken. Remarkably, they were not matched to his fugitive record at the time, and the charges were dropped, allowing him to continue his double life unchecked. Had the fingerprint match been discovered then, his time as a fugitive would have been cut short by twelve years.

By early 2005, J.J. Jameson's double life had endured for nearly twenty years. However, he had developed serious medical issues, including head tumors that affected his health. In late 2004, he underwent jaw surgery, and his appearances at poetry events became sporadic. A reading in February 2005 at a local coffee shop was something of a "comeback" after illness—it would be his final performance as a free man.

For two decades, Massachusetts authorities had hunted Norman Porter with little success. He remained at the very top of the state's "Most Wanted" list, but Porter's ability to blend in and the lack of digital records in the 1980s made the trail go cold.

A breakthrough came in early 2005. Acting on a tip from an informant in Massachusetts, investigators revisited old clues. They discovered that Porter's fingerprints from the 1993 Chicago arrest were sitting in an FBI file, unnoticed for twelve years. In 2005, Detective Michael Pepe received an FBI form letter indicating a fingerprint match for Norman Porter under the Jameson alias. Armed with this knowledge, Pepe simply plugged the name "J.J. Jameson" into an internet search engine. Porter's carefully constructed new life was laid bare; the search results showed Jameson as a prominent Chicago poet, even Poet of the Month on a local poetry website, complete with a photo.

Investigators were stunned that Porter had been hiding in plain sight online. They coordinated with Illinois authorities and put together a plan to apprehend him without tipping him off. On March 22, 2005, a team of officers descended on Chicago. They knew Jameson was involved with the Third Unitarian Church, so they started their search there, using a ruse of showing a random photograph and asking if anyone had seen the man in the photo.

When Jameson himself walked into the church office that morning, the officers recognized him immediately. After confirming his alias, they placed him under arrest. The guise of J.J. Jameson shattered in an instant. As they walked him out of the church in handcuffs, Porter sighed and said, "Well, I've had a good twenty years." He did not resist arrest.

The news of Norman Porter's capture made national headlines. "Escaped Killer Hid as Poet in Chicago," as one headline put it. Porter was promptly extradited back to Massachusetts under heavy guard, and reactions from Chicago friends were a mix of shock, disbelief, and retrospective clarity. C.J. Laity, a local poetry website editor who had championed Jameson, said he "broke out in goosebumps" when he learned his friend's true identity. "It was just startling—it was J.J. Jameson, a man you thought you knew," Laity told reporters. "You find out it's true: He blew a guy's head off with a shotgun, and you invited him into your home. It's very scary."

In Boston and Saugus, news of Porter's capture was met with a sense of justice long delayed. The Robinson family, who had never been notified of Porter's 1975 commutation and had spent decades grappling with the loss of David Robinson, expressed both relief and renewed grief at the news. Robinson's grandson later testified how their family had been left with only memories, a medal, and a badge to remember the jail master who died simply doing his duty. Claire Wilcox, John Pigott's former fiancée, said, "All these people have had to live forty-five years knowing this guy was out there. He's had twenty years of playtime. It's time he finished his sentence."

After his return to Massachusetts, Porter faced legal consequences for the 1985 escape. In October 2005, he pleaded guilty to the escape charge and received an additional three-year sentence to be served consecutively after his life term. This meant Porter's earliest parole hearing wouldn't come until 2009.

Porter was now in his mid-60s and had returned to a high-security prison environment after two decades of freedom. Unlike his earlier prison stint, Porter did not involve himself in the many institutional programs this time—perhaps due to age, or maybe a sense that he had already proven himself to be rehabilitated in the outside world.

In 2008, a documentary film titled "Killer Poet" premiered, chronicling Porter's double life and highlighting the reform vs. justice dilemma that his case embodied. The film influenced public perception as his parole hearings approached.

Porter became eligible for parole in late 2009. A group called "Friends of Norman Porter" argued that he had reformed himself during his twenty years in Chicago. They pointed to his good deeds, his role as a church leader and poet, and claimed he exemplified the ideals of rehabilitation.

On the other side stood the families of Porter's victims, who vehemently opposed parole. The Massachusetts Parole Board denied his request in November 2009, noting that Porter showed insufficient remorse and had not engaged in available prison programs since his return. They issued a five-year setback.

In January 2015, seventy-four-year-old Porter went before the parole board for the second time. Though he offered what he called a sincere apology, Porter somewhat minimized his responsibility, noting, "I didn't kill anyone," referring to not being the triggerman in Robinson's case. To the victims' families, this rang hollow. Dottie Johnson, Pigott's cousin, said bluntly: "His remorse is self-centered. He is sorry he got caught." The board again denied parole.

Porter was denied parole a third time in 2019. By then, his health was failing severely. In 2022, at age eighty-two, he applied for medical parole, a provision for terminally ill inmates. Porter was suffering from congestive heart failure, chronic lung disease, and was nearly deaf and blind. The Massachusetts Parole Board unanimously granted his request, noting the extraordinary circumstance: "We don't need to wonder whether Porter could live a relatively harmless life outside prison. He already has."

Norman Porter was released after seventeen years back inside (and forty-two total years behind bars when adding his original term). He lived quietly under parole supervision for about a year and a half. On December 27, 2023, Porter died at the age of eighty-three from natural causes.

CHAPTER 9
THE BATHTUB KILLER

The city of Arlington, Texas, sits nestled between Dallas and Fort Worth in the heart of the Metroplex. By 1996, the population had grown to nearly 300,000, making it the third-largest city in the area, and the Peartree Apartments complex was like many other suburban developments. A collection of moderately priced units populated by young professionals, students, and working-class families, with manicured lawns and tidy walkways, it projected an image of safety and normalcy.

All of that changed on September 17, 1996.

Twenty-five-year-old Christine Vu, an elementary school teacher, was preparing for her day when her long-time boyfriend, Thang Khuu, left for work. Christine had a busy schedule ahead of her, starting with her morning classes. When Khuu returned to the apartment that afternoon, he found the front door locked from the inside. After knocking several times without a response, he left briefly to call Christine's workplace and her mother, concerned by her silence. When he returned a short time later, the door was unexpectedly unlocked. He stepped inside, and what he found would haunt him forever.

Christine's nude body lay face down in the bathroom, submerged in a half-filled bathtub. In a panic, Khuu pulled her lifeless body from the water and into the living room, but it was far too late.

Police arrived to find Christine beyond help. Her body had been bound with duct tape around her wrists, ankles, and neck in a hog-tied position. Tape also covered her mouth. The autopsy would later confirm the horrific details. Christine had been raped, manually strangled, and then drowned. Her killer had held her bound body underwater until she'd stopped breathing.

Investigators initially questioned Khuu, as partners are often the first suspects in such cases. However, they quickly cleared him when forensic evidence didn't implicate him, and his timeline for the day checked out. In fact, detectives theorized that while Khuu was outside the apartment after finding the door locked, the killer had most likely been inside with Christine's body, waiting for an opportunity to slip away unnoticed.

Crime scene technicians processed the apartment meticulously. Beyond Christine's body and the tape used to bind her, they found little physical evidence. However, they did recover a single latent fingerprint from inside the apartment and collected DNA evidence from Christine's body. With no immediate suspect, the prints and DNA were entered into law enforcement databases, but in 1996, these searches yielded no matches.

The Arlington community was shocked by the brutal murder, but the horror was just beginning.

Three months later, on Christmas Eve, another tragedy struck the very same apartment complex. Twenty-year-old Wendie Prescott, a well-liked teacher's aide from nearby Mansfield, had failed to show up for a planned shopping trip with her sister. Concerned family members went to check on her at her home in Peartree Apartments—the same building as Christine Vu.

Around 11:00 p.m., Wendie's uncle, Norman Norwood, made the nightmarish discovery. Like Christine, Wendie's body lay face down in a half-filled bathtub. She was naked, bound with duct tape in the same distinctive hog-tied fashion—wrists, ankles, and neck wrapped tightly with a length of tape connecting them down her back. The medical examiner would later conclude that she had been sexually assaulted and died from manual strangulation, possibly combined with drowning from being left in the water.

The pattern was unmistakable. Two young women, both found in half-filled bathtubs, both bound with duct tape, both raped and strangled. Both lived just steps from each other in the same apartment complex. News media quickly dubbed the perpetrator the "Bathtub Killer," and residents of Peartree Apartments began moving out in droves.

"You don't have concern. You've got absolute panic," recalled Arlington Detective Tommy LeNoir of the atmosphere in late 1996.

Investigators working on Wendie's murder found one promising lead: a high-quality fingerprint impression left in dust on her TV stand. This print, along with DNA samples from her body, was carefully collected as evidence. Initial fingerprint checks in state and FBI databases came up empty—the print did not match any known offender on record in 1996. Similarly, the DNA from both crime scenes did not match anyone in the existing DNA indexes at the time.

With no immediate leads, both the Vu and Prescott cases went cold, frustrating detectives and terrifying the public. As months passed with no arrests, rumors swirled that a serial killer might still be lurking in Arlington.

For the next several weeks, police conducted extensive interviews with residents and maintenance staff at the Peartree Apartments. They compiled a list of male occupants who had been present during both murders, carefully checked alibis, and looked into anyone who might have had access to both victims' units. They canvassed the neighborhood, questioned known sex offenders in the area, and reviewed recent parolees—all to no avail.

Throughout 1997, the case remained at a standstill. No new murders matching the "bathtub" pattern occurred, leading some to wonder if the killer had moved on or been imprisoned for another crime. The community remained vigilant, but as time passed without new attacks, the acute fear began to wane.

While the bathtub murders had stopped after Wendie Prescott, a new pattern of violence emerged in the region. Between 1998 and 1999, a series of sexual assaults occurred across the Dallas-Fort Worth area. The attacker's method was consistent—breaking into women's apartments at night, raping and beating them, but leaving them alive.

On September 21, 1998, a woman was raped in her apartment in Grand Prairie, a city between Dallas and Arlington. The victim was ambushed at home and sexually assaulted, with DNA evidence collected from her rape kit. At the time, investigators had no suspect, but the DNA would later prove crucial.

Just eleven days later, on October 2, a Dallas police officer was attacked after returning home from her shift. The assailant surprised her in her apartment, sexually assaulted her, and fled. Notably, this officer lived only yards from the September victim, suggesting the attacker was targeting a specific area or complex. This attack on a law enforcement officer deeply rattled the police community, though her identity was protected in public reports.

Two months later, on December 18, another woman was raped in her apartment in Lancaster, Texas, south of Dallas. Again, a sexual assault forensic exam yielded DNA evidence that would later be vital to the investigation.

On February 23, 1999, twenty-two-year-old college student Chima Benson awoke in the middle of the night to find a man straddling her in her sorority house near the University of Texas at Arlington.

He said, "Don't scream, and I won't kill you," Benson later recalled.

The intruder brutally beat her and forced her to perform sexual acts. In a desperate act of resistance, Chima bit her attacker's genitals hard during the assault. Enraged, he pistol-whipped and punched her severely, then raped her again and left her for dead on the floor. Against all odds, Chima survived the attack. Her description of the rapist and the injury she inflicted would later prove pivotal in identifying her attacker.

Eight months later, on October 26, another woman in Arlington was raped in her apartment after going to sleep. Like the others, she was ambushed in the night by an intruder who seemed to know exactly when and where to strike.

All five women survived their ordeals, though they were left deeply traumatized. The attacker in each case was described as an African American male who assaulted them in the early morning hours. He subdued victims with physical force or threats of a weapon and sometimes bound or attempted to bind them, though not always with the elaborate duct tape method used in the murders.

At the time, each of these new cases was investigated in its own jurisdiction, and the connection with the Arlington murders wasn't immediately recognized.

Meanwhile, the Arlington murder cases had gone cold. Despite thorough investigations—interviewing neighbors, checking local sex offenders, and processing every piece of evidence—detectives had no name to attach to the fingerprint or DNA from the crime scenes. Detectives simply had two eerily similar murders and a nameless suspect. Investigators were stumped. The forensic evidence was solid, but it pointed to an unknown person.

In May 1999, a man named Dale Devon Scheanette was arrested for a completely unrelated crime—burglary of a car audio store in DeSoto, Texas. He was convicted of criminal mischief and sentenced to a year in jail. During this arrest, his fingerprints were taken and entered into the criminal database. At the time, no one connected this minor offender to the Arlington murders, but it planted the seed for the case breakthrough: Scheanette's prints were now on file, awaiting a match.

By mid-2000, Arlington cold-case detectives decided to rerun the fingerprints from the Wendie Prescott crime scene through the improved Automated Fingerprint Identification System (AFIS). Technology had advanced, and the database had grown substantially in the four years since the murders. This time, they got a hit.

That summer, an FBI fingerprint analyst reported back with stunning news: The unknown print from Wendie Prescott's TV stand matched the known print of Dale Devon Scheanette. The FBI's system gave the match a very high confidence score—2,500 points, significantly higher than the next possible candidate. Arlington detectives manually verified the match and agreed. After nearly four years, they finally had a name.

Who was Dale Devon Scheanette? Born on May 7, 1973, in Ouachita Parish, Louisiana, he relocated to Texas in the 1990s as a young adult. By all accounts, he experienced an ordinary childhood and came from what his defense attorneys later described as a "good family unit." In Texas, he held various blue-collar jobs—working as a machine operator, warehouseman, and forklift operator. By 1996, he had married and was living in Arlington.

Dale Devon Scheanette

Scheanette had no significant criminal record before his spree of violence, explaining why his fingerprints weren't in any database during the initial investigation. There was nothing in his known background—neither a troubled past nor a history of violence—that hinted at the predator he would become.

Once Scheanette was identified, Arlington Police, joined by Texas Rangers, moved quickly. Surveillance was initiated to ensure he didn't flee, and investigators gathered more information. They discovered a key detail: Scheanette had indeed lived in Peartree Apartments in 1996, placing him at the scene of both murders. He was a neighbor of the women he had killed.

With a suspect identified, detectives obtained a warrant to collect Scheanette's DNA. In September 2000, officers arrested him during a traffic stop to avoid tipping him off and took a saliva swab for genetic testing. The crime lab compared Scheanette's DNA profile to the sperm samples from Wendie Prescott's autopsy. The results were conclusive beyond any reasonable doubt: Scheanette's DNA matched the samples with astronomical certainty. It was a scientific certainty that Scheanette had raped Wendie Prescott and left his DNA behind. They ran the same comparison with Christine Vu's autopsy samples and, again, got a match to Scheanette.

Armed with his DNA profile, analysts then compared it to the backlog of unsolved sexual assault kits from 1998–99 in the area. One by one, those five cases lit up with matches. The DNA from each assault matched Dale Devon Scheanette. This conclusively tied him to seven separate attacks on women—the two murders and five rapes. Law enforcement now understood the full scope of his crime spree.

A particularly telling piece of corroborative evidence emerged thanks to Chima Benson's brave resistance. After Scheanette's arrest, investigators obtained a warrant to examine his body. They discovered a scar on his genital area consistent with a healed human bite mark, exactly where Chima had bitten her attacker months earlier. This provided a unique piece of evidence linking Scheanette to Chima's account of the assault.

Forensic science played a crucial role in solving this case. Fingerprint evidence provided the initial breakthrough, and DNA evidence sealed it shut.

Tarrant County prosecutors charged Scheanette with the death of Wendie Prescott—capital murder, because it was murder in the course of committing another felony, sexual assault. Although Scheanette was also indicted for Christine Vu's murder, the decision was made to try the Prescott case first and hold the Vu case in reserve, a common strategy in such proceedings.

The capital murder trial for Wendie Prescott's slaying began in January 2003 in Fort Worth, Texas. It had been just over six years since the crime. Media coverage was significant, with local reporters noting the community's eagerness for justice.

During opening statements, prosecutor Greg Miller outlined the forensic evidence tying Scheanette to the crime, especially the fingerprint and DNA. Surprisingly, the defense chose to defer its opening statement, offering no immediate rebuttal after the state's presentation. This suggested they had few ways to counter the hard forensic facts and would instead focus on sparing Scheanette's life.

Key witnesses included Norman Norwood, who testified about finding his niece's body on Christmas Eve 1996. His emotional account set the tone, showing the human toll of the crime. Norwood later told reporters he was relieved the trial had finally started and that he wanted to see the face of the man who killed his niece.

Crime scene technicians presented photographs of Wendie Prescott's apartment as it was found. Jurors were shown graphic crime scene photos: Wendie's body as it was discovered in the tub, the duct tape bindings, and the lifted fingerprint enlarged for comparison.

Forensic experts testified that the latent print from the scene matched Dale Scheanette's fingerprint. A DNA analyst from the state crime lab then testified about the DNA match, explaining the 1 in 763 million odds and effectively identifying Scheanette as the source of semen in Wendie's body.

Confronted with this overwhelming evidence, Scheanette's defense attorneys had a daunting task. They argued that the evidence was circumstantial and attempted to poke holes in it where possible. They questioned the handling of the fingerprint and posed the possibility that the DNA could have been contaminated. However, these arguments rang hollow given the breadth of forensic links.

After less than a day of deliberation, the jury found Dale Devon Scheanette guilty of capital murder for Wendie Prescott's death. With guilt established, the trial moved to the punishment phase, where the same jury was tasked with deciding whether Scheanette should be put to death or spend the rest of his life in prison without parole.

During the sentencing phase, the prosecution repeated the full story of Scheanette's criminal rampage to argue that he posed a future danger and deserved the death penalty.

They called five women to the stand—the survivors of Scheanette's rapes—to give heart-wrenching testimony about what he had done to them. One by one, these women recounted how Scheanette broke into their homes, beat them, threatened their lives, and sexually assaulted them. They detailed the terror of those encounters—being awakened by a stranger, the threats, and the physical injuries they sustained.

The courtroom was tense and emotional. Several jurors were seen tearing up as the victims spoke. After their testimony, the five women, who had never met one another before, cried and hugged one another outside the courtroom—a therapeutic moment of shared survival.

Their collective stories painted Scheanette as a vicious serial rapist of the worst order—one who would likely continue hurting women if ever given the chance.

Prosecutors also introduced evidence of Scheanette's behavior while in custody. They highlighted an incident where jailers found a plexiglass shank hidden in his cell, implying he was plotting violence even behind bars. They reminded jurors that Scheanette had a prior burglary conviction—not a violent crime, per se, but something that showed a pattern of lawbreaking. All of this was meant to show that Scheanette would continue to be a danger to others, even behind bars, and should be sentenced to death instead of life in prison.

The defense tried to humanize Scheanette. They brought several of his family members to testify, who pleaded for mercy and described him in gentler terms—as a son, brother, and friend who had the potential for good. A chaplain who knew Scheanette spoke on his behalf, and a retired Texas prison employee testified about the strict security measures in prison, suggesting that Scheanette could be managed in a prison environment for life without incident. Despite these efforts, the aggravating evidence was simply too compelling.

After deliberating, the jury made its decision. In January 2003, Dale Devon Scheanette was formally sentenced to death by lethal injection for the capital murder of Wendie Prescott. As the verdict was read, Wendie's family held hands and quietly thanked the jurors. Scheanette himself showed little emotion.

The second murder charge for Christine Vu's murder remained pending, but prosecutors later announced they would not pursue a separate trial since the death sentence was secured. He was charged but never tried for the killing. This spared Christine's family the ordeal of another trial while knowing that justice had effectively been achieved.

Detectives saw in Scheanette a man who enjoyed inflicting terror and pain. The fact that he escalated to murder, then continued sexually assaulting women for years afterward, showed an unabated compulsion to dominate victims.

Yet his decision not to kill the later victims might indicate a calculating side—perhaps he knew a murder would dramatically increase police resources and media attention on his case. By "only" raping and not killing in 1998–99, he could more easily fly under the radar, as sexual assaults didn't get the same headlines as homicides.

In the years after his conviction, Scheanette's case went through the standard appeals process. The Texas Court of Criminal Appeals affirmed his conviction and death sentence in September 2004, finding no reversible error in the trial. The U.S. Supreme Court declined to review the case in 2005. Scheanette then pursued both state and federal habeas corpus relief, raising numerous claims—ineffective counsel, issues with jury instructions, etc. These were ultimately denied. In March 2007, the U.S. Fifth Circuit Court of Appeals rejected his final appeal, moving him closer to an execution date.

During his years on Texas's Death Row at the Polunsky Unit, Scheanette was mostly a silent figure. He declined interview requests from the media as his execution neared. There was no public show of remorse, nor extensive efforts to plead for clemency.

In a last-ditch move, his sister sent a handwritten motion to the U.S. Supreme Court on the day of execution asking for a stay, but it was denied within hours.

On February 10, 2009, more than twelve years after the murders, Dale Devon Scheanette was executed by lethal injection at the Texas State Penitentiary in Huntsville. He was thirty-five years old. Witnesses to the execution included six relatives of Christine Vu and Wendie Prescott, who gathered to watch the monster who had murdered their loved ones take his last breath.

Asked if he had any final statement, Scheanette paused and simply said: "My only statement is that no cases ever tried have been error-free. Those are my words. No cases are error-free."

It was an odd and defiant final statement—rather than apologizing, he seemed to suggest his trial was flawed, though courts had found otherwise. He did not acknowledge or look at the victims' family members who were present. At 6:21 p.m., Scheanette was pronounced dead. In Texas's busy execution schedule, he was the seventh person executed in the state that year.

After his death, the detectives who worked the case couldn't help but wonder if there were other victims of Scheanette out there. Given the gap between 1996 and 1998, or any period before 1996 when Scheanette was an adult, the possibility remains that he may have assaulted other women who never reported it or whose cases remain unsolved.

Two of Scheanette's surviving victims later chose to speak out publicly, turning their trauma into advocacy and personal strength. Chima Benson (later known as Chima Simone), after recovering from her injuries, went on to appear on the reality TV show Big Brother. She used that platform to tell the world about surviving the "Bathtub Killer" and to encourage other women to fight back and report sexual violence. Adrienne Fields likewise shared her story years later, giving interviews about how she sensed the danger and how she endured the assault, hoping to help others recognize and trust their instincts in potentially dangerous situations.

The "Bathtub Killer" case became an example in law enforcement circles of the value of preserving evidence and periodically re-running prints and DNA through evolving technology. The fact that a fingerprint resubmission in 2000 solved a 1996 double murder served as a showcase of AFIS improvements. It showed how patience, persistence, and scientific advances could eventually bring justice, even when a predator seemed to have gotten away with murder.

CHAPTER 10
CHILD OF CHAOS

The coastal town of Ipswich, Suffolk, sits quietly on England's eastern shore. With a population of around 135,000, it's known for its historic waterfront, medieval churches, and as the birthplace of Cardinal Wolsey. Beneath the surface of this seemingly ordinary town, however, lies a darker reality.

Away from the tourist spots and historic sites, a different kind of life plays out in the town's rougher neighborhoods—one that most residents prefer not to acknowledge. In these forgotten pockets of Ipswich, groups gather daily in dingy flats or on street corners. They're the town's invisible residents, living day-to-day, focused primarily on where their next drink will come from. Most townsfolk simply walk past them, averting their eyes and continuing their normal lives.

But in the summer of 2009, events would unfold in this hidden community that would force all of Ipswich—and indeed all of Britain—to confront a horror they could never have imagined.

Born in 1994, Lorraine Thorpe had little chance of normalcy from the beginning. Her early childhood in Ipswich was marked by extreme poverty and instability. Her parents separated when she was around twelve years old, and although she initially lived with her mother, Lorraine chose to move in with her father, Desmond Thorpe, when she was thirteen.

The choice would prove fateful. Desmond was a severe alcoholic with debilitating health problems. At forty-three, he couldn't walk without assistance and required constant care. Despite his issues, there was love between father and daughter. Lorraine took on the role of caretaker for her father, a responsibility far beyond what any child should bear.

Their living situation was dire. They moved frequently between squalid flats and occasionally lived in tents. More critically, their daily life exposed Lorraine to a dangerous social circle—adults who gathered daily to drink, often engaging in petty crime and violence.

By the time she was thirteen, Lorraine had stopped attending school. She had been diagnosed with attention deficit hyperactivity disorder (ADHD) but wasn't taking her medication regularly. Suffolk Social Services were aware of her precarious situation and made multiple attempts to intervene, but Lorraine repeatedly ran away from any structure they tried to impose, always returning to her father's side.

In this dysfunctional environment, Lorraine's moral compass never properly developed. She became accustomed to seeing fights and lawlessness as everyday occurrences. By fifteen, she had become stubborn and willful beyond her years. She was known to be manipulative and quick to resort to aggression.

By 2009, Lorraine was on the run from social services, evading their attempts to place her in a safer environment. She was living full-time in an adult world where violence and chaos were the norm.

Among the hard-drinking crowd that Lorraine frequented was forty-one-year-old Paul Clarke. Described as a bully and the dominant figure among the group, Clarke exerted significant influence over the people around him. Despite the twenty-six-year age gap between them, Lorraine became drawn to Clarke.

Some accounts suggested Clarke was her older boyfriend, though the exact nature of their relationship remained unclear. What was evident was that Lorraine became besotted with Clarke. She craved his approval and attention, and she would do almost anything to impress him.

Their dynamic was complex. While Clarke was certainly the dominant influence, Lorraine wasn't simply a puppet. She had her own cruel streak and was capable of being highly manipulative herself.

Clarke had previously been in a relationship with a woman named Rosalyn "Rosie" Hunt, another woman in her forties who moved in the same circles. The relationship had deteriorated, and by the summer of 2009, tensions were building between Clarke and Hunt.

The catalyst appeared to be an incident involving a dog. According to court reports, Clarke became enraged because Rosalyn had allowed a dog to attack a child within their community. This dispute sparked a serious falling out.

Lorraine, fiercely loyal to Clarke and eager to prove herself, sided with him in this conflict. By early August 2009, their anger toward Rosalyn Hunt had escalated to dangerous levels, setting the stage for what would become a horrific series of events.

Forty-one-year-old Rosalyn Hunt was a mother of two who lived in the same world of street drinking as Lorraine and Clarke. In early August 2009, she became the target of their building rage.

After the quarrel involving Rosalyn's dog, Clarke and Lorraine decided to "teach her a lesson." In the first days of August, they went to Rosalyn's flat—the place she called home—and refused to leave.

What followed was truly horrific. Over a period of several days, Rosalyn Hunt was subjected to sustained, sadistic torture. She was held captive and brutalized in her own home.

The torture was relentless. Lorraine and Clarke beat Rosalyn mercilessly—kicking, punching, and stomping on her again and again. Autopsy findings would later reveal that Rosalyn suffered multiple broken bones, including at least nine broken ribs.

But the abuse went far beyond beating. According to court reports, the torture included grotesque, sadistic acts using various implements. They whipped her with a dog leash chain. They cruelly rubbed a cheese grater against her skin. They poured salt into her wounds to maximize her pain. At one point, they even set her hair on fire.

For days, this nightmare continued. Rosalyn was badly injured, likely incapacitated, and unable to defend herself. Neither Lorraine nor Clarke showed her mercy. In mid-August 2009, after more than a week of intermittent torture, Rosalyn Hunt succumbed to her injuries. She had been beaten to death.

A heartbreaking aspect of this case was the missed opportunity to save Rosalyn. On August 4, 2009, someone called 999 (the UK emergency number) to report a disturbance at Rosalyn's residence. Suffolk police officers responded and knocked on the door, but they received no answer. After checking around the property and seeing no obvious signs of trouble, they left without forcing entry.

At that time, Rosalyn was likely inside, possibly badly hurt and unable to call out. Whether she was still alive on August 4 remains uncertain, but the police missed a chance to intervene.

It was only five days later, on August 9, when a neighbor noticed Rosalyn hadn't been seen for days and that the authorities were contacted again. This time, officers forced their way into the flat and discovered her battered body on the floor. She had died from multiple injuries due to continuous attacks.

Far from showing remorse, Lorraine apparently boasted about the attack to friends. According to court testimony, she "gloried in it, describing to her friends how she stamped on Rosalyn's head." This chilling bravado from a schoolgirl shocked even hardened detectives.

With Rosalyn Hunt dead, Lorraine and Clarke now faced a problem: Desmond Thorpe, Lorraine's father, knew too much. He was aware of their social circle and could potentially implicate them in Rosalyn's death. To cover their tracks, they decided Desmond had to be eliminated as well.

Around August 9 or 10—just as Rosalyn's body was being discovered—Lorraine and Clarke carried out the second murder. The method was different this time. Instead of prolonged torture, Desmond was executed swiftly: Lorraine and Clarke suffocated him by pressing a cushion or pillow over his face until he stopped breathing.

Physically weak and dependent on his daughter for care, Desmond couldn't fight back. While Clarke likely took the lead, Lorraine was an active participant in her father's murder. After they smothered him, she assaulted his body, even striking his head, similar to what she had done to Rosalyn.

In a chilling detail, Lorraine later told police investigators that they would find the imprint of her shoe on her father's head. Just as she had said, Desmond's face bore the evidence of Lorraine's shoe tread.

The betrayal here was profound. Desmond Thorpe was so debilitated that he was unable to walk unaided or do anything for himself. He was completely defenseless, and the very person entrusted with his care—his teenage daughter—had helped kill him.

With Desmond dead, Lorraine and Clarke likely thought they had covered their tracks. However, their attempts at concealment would soon unravel, bringing the full horror of their crimes to light.

The discovery of Rosalyn Hunt's battered body on August 9, 2009, triggered an intensive police investigation. Within twenty-four hours, law enforcement had zeroed in on suspects. On August 10, Suffolk police arrested Lorraine Thorpe and Paul Clarke on suspicion of murder. A third man, twenty-seven-year-old John Grimwood, who was part of the same street-drinking group, was also taken into custody.

As investigators pieced together the timeline, they realized they were dealing with two homicides likely perpetrated by the same people. Physical evidence and witness statements quickly built a compelling case.

Witnesses from the drinking community came forward. Some had heard Lorraine bragging about hurting Rosalyn, while others had overheard the pair with Hunt during the days of her captivity. Forensic evidence linked the suspects to both victims. In Desmond's case, the evidence was particularly direct—the shoe impression on his face did, indeed, match Lorraine's footwear.

By late August 2009, the investigation had gathered enough evidence for formal charges. On August 25, Lorraine Thorpe and Paul Clarke were charged with two counts of murder. John Grimwood was charged specifically with Rosalyn's murder.

The UK press quickly picked up on the case, particularly noting Lorraine's young age. Headlines referred to her as potentially the youngest female involved in such crimes, drawing comparisons to rare historical cases like Mary Bell, who killed two toddlers at age eleven in 1968, and Sharon Carr, who committed murder at age twelve in 1992.

Meanwhile, police continued to investigate their earlier response to the 999 call at Rosalyn's flat. The Independent Police Complaints Commission (IPCC) launched an inquiry to determine if officers had done all they reasonably should have that night. The possibility that Rosalyn might have been saved with a more thorough response haunted the investigation.

Throughout the inquiry, Lorraine and Clarke maintained their innocence and refused to cooperate. Their strategy was simply to deny involvement and provide no testimony to counter the mounting evidence against them.

The trial of Lorraine Thorpe and Paul Clarke began in mid-2010 at Ipswich Crown Court, with Mr. Justice Saunders presiding. Because Lorraine was a minor, special considerations applied, including restrictions on the media naming her until conviction. Still, the proceedings drew intense interest due to the shocking nature of the crimes and the youth of one defendant.

Both Lorraine and Clarke pleaded not guilty to the murders. Throughout the trial, they denied the charges and gave no evidence in their own defense. Neither chose to testify, forcing the prosecution to prove the case solely with evidence. There was no visible remorse or explanation from the accused—just silence in the face of horrific accusations.

The prosecution laid out the horrific story of how Rosalyn Hunt had been sadistically tortured and killed and how Lorraine's father, Desmond Thorpe, was smothered days later to cover up the first crime. The jury learned of

Rosalyn's broken ribs, her captivity and beatings, and how, by the end of those attacks, she was completely helpless.

When it came to the murder of Desmond Thorpe, the prosecution explained how vulnerable he had been—an immobile alcoholic killed by the daughter who should have protected him. Medical testimony described how he had died by smothering, with the added indignity of being stomped after death.

The court also heard evidence of Lorraine's disturbing attitude toward the violence. Witnesses recounted her bragging about the attacks. Unlike a frightened child coerced by an adult, the prosecution portrayed Lorraine as an eager participant who derived fun and entertainment from extreme brutality.

After hearing all the evidence, the jury returned with its verdict in August 2010. Paul Clarke and Lorraine Thorpe, now sixteen, were found guilty on all counts. The third defendant, John Grimwood, was acquitted.

On September 7, 2010, sentencing took place at the Old Bailey in London. Justice Saunders delivered a damning assessment of both defendants.

Paul Clarke, having already been sentenced a month earlier, received life imprisonment with a minimum term of twenty-seven years before parole eligibility. In effect, Clarke was to be locked up until at least his late sixties, if not for the rest of his life.

For Lorraine, the judge had to balance her youth against the severity of her crimes. "Her story is an appalling one, and her case is rightly described as wholly exceptional," he said. Justice Saunders acknowledged her extremely dysfunctional background but made it clear that such circumstances couldn't excuse the heinous acts she had committed.

Lorraine Thorpe was ordered to be detained for life, with a minimum tariff of fourteen years. This meant she would not even be considered for release until she had served fourteen years and demonstrated significant rehabilitation—and even then, release would depend on approval by the Parole Board.

In his sentencing remarks, Justice Saunders carefully detailed Lorraine's dual nature: a product of a terrible environment, yet also a willing perpetrator. He noted that there was "no doubt she cared for and loved her father" on some level, making her participation in his murder all the more disturbing.

He identified Paul Clarke as the instigator, calling him the dominant partner in crime, but noting Lorraine played a full part in everything that happened. She was not dragged along unwillingly; she embraced the violence. The judge highlighted how Lorraine had delighted in kicking, punching, and stomping on Rosalyn during the torture.

He also commented on how violence had become a form of entertainment for the young girl. Lorraine had become numb to the suffering of others—a likely result of having seen so much violence growing up, but also indicating a deeply disturbed mindset.

As the sentence was handed down, Lorraine Thorpe entered the annals of British crime history as the nation's youngest female double murderer. Headlines blared the news across the country, and the public reacted with horror and disgust at how a child could go so wrong.

Lorraine Thorpe and Paul Clarke both appealed their convictions, as was their right. In April 2011, the case went before the Court of Appeal. The exact grounds of their appeal weren't fully detailed in reports, but they likely challenged the strength of evidence, particularly for Desmond Thorpe's murder.

On April 14, 2011, the appeal was swiftly rejected. The appellate judges upheld the conviction and sentences, finding no miscarriage of justice in how the trial was conducted or in the jury's verdict. Lorraine's life sentence remained intact, and any hope of an early release was quashed.

For Paul Clarke, prison life would be brief. On September 1, 2014, news broke that Clarke had been found dead in his cell at HMP Whitemoor, a maximum-security prison. The forty-six-year-old was discovered unresponsive early that morning. Authorities released very few details, but there were no indications of foul play. Clarke likely died by suicide or from health issues related to years of excessive alcohol abuse. He hadn't completed even a fifth of his twenty-seven-year term.

Lorraine continued to serve her sentence. Initially, she was held in a youth offenders institution until she was later transferred to an adult women's prison. Records indicate she was eventually housed at HM Prison Foston Hall, where she joined other notorious female inmates.

Behind bars, Lorraine reportedly participated in various rehabilitation programs. She engaged in courses aimed at addressing her decision-making and understanding risk factors, as well as programs dealing with substance abuse. These efforts would be crucial for any future bid for release.

After serving her fourteen-year minimum tariff, Lorraine Thorpe became eligible for parole consideration in 2023. In October of that year, the Parole Board convened to assess her case. However, Lorraine herself chose not to take part in the parole process, suggesting she either felt unready or believed her release was unlikely to be approved.

The Parole Board refused to release Lorraine or even move her to an open prison setting. In their statement, they emphasized that Lorraine was still deemed too great a risk to be released. They cited ongoing risk factors associated with her case, including her early life experiences and past substance abuse. While she had made some progress through prison programs, the board felt she needed to do more work to address these issues.

With parole denied, Lorraine Thorpe remains incarcerated today. As of the latest updates, no specific release date is on the horizon, and she continues to serve her life sentence.

Lorraine Thorpe's case raises pressing questions about nature, nurture, and criminal responsibility. What could drive a fifteen-year-old girl to commit such barbaric acts?

Her upbringing clearly had a profound psychological impact. From her early teens, she observed and experienced a world where physical fights and cruelty were commonplace. The adults she knew modeled dysfunctional, antisocial behavior, and over time, Lorraine became desensitized to violence. It was everyday life for her.

Lorraine also displayed traits of callousness and manipulation. She seemed to get enjoyment from violence. Multiple sources noted that she found cruelty funny and entertaining;

laughing and bragging about stomping someone's head suggests a disturbing lack of empathy.

The influence of Paul Clarke was undoubtedly a significant factor. Lorraine was smitten with the man and eager to please. In the chaotic life she led, Clarke might have represented a figure of power or even affection. To gain his approval, she was willing to go to extremes.

As of this writing, Lorraine Thorpe is thirty years old—double the age she was when she committed these crimes. Whether she can ever be rehabilitated remains an open question, but the Parole Board's decision to keep her incarcerated suggests that they believe she still poses a significant threat to society.

CHAPTER 11
HE NEEDED KILLING

Skidmore, Missouri, was a typical Midwestern farming community where people tended to mind their own business and keep to themselves. With a population hovering around 435 in 1980, it was the kind of tiny town where everyone knew one another's affairs, whether they wanted to or not. Nestled among the rolling corn and soybean fields of Nodaway County in the northwest corner of the state, the town had one main street, a handful of businesses, and a quiet pace of life that rarely attracted outside attention.

For decades, the people of Skidmore had lived by an unspoken code of rural self-reliance. If someone's barn needed raising, neighbors showed up without being asked. If a family fell on hard times, food appeared on their doorstep. And when trouble came calling, folks handled it themselves whenever possible, preferring not to involve outsiders or authorities any more than necessary.

This quiet community had its fair share of good people. Hardworking farmers who rose before dawn to tend their fields, shopkeepers who extended credit during lean times, and families who had lived on the same land for generations. But amid this setting of ordinary small-town life, one man stood apart—not for his goodness, but for the cloud of fear that followed him wherever he went.

His name was Ken McElroy.

Ken Rex McElroy entered the world on June 1, 1934, as the fifteenth of sixteen children born to Tony and Mabel McElroy. The family lived in extreme poverty, working as migrant tenant farmers before eventually settling on the outskirts of Skidmore. From an early age, it was clear that Ken wouldn't follow the straight and narrow path. He dropped out of school in the eighth grade at age fifteen, barely literate but street-smart in ways that would serve his criminal tendencies.

Even as a teenager, McElroy's imposing physical presence made him intimidating. Standing at over six feet tall and eventually weighing around 270 pounds, he had thick, dark eyebrows that seemed perpetually furrowed in anger, piercing blue eyes, and a hair-trigger temper that could explode at the slightest provocation. Those who knew him in his youth recalled a boy who was quick to solve problems with his fists and showed little regard for rules or authority.

The young McElroy quickly discovered that his size and temperament could get him what he wanted. By his late teens, he had developed a reputation for petty theft, hunting out of season, and general mischief that gradually escalated into more serious crimes. Despite having little formal education or legitimate employment, McElroy always seemed to have cash on hand—wads of hundred-dollar bills that he carried loosely in his pocket and flashed around town.

"He never had a job that I knew of," recalled one longtime Skidmore resident. "But he always had money."

That money came from a variety of illegal enterprises that McElroy ran throughout Nodaway County and the surrounding area. Cattle rustling became his primary trade: He stole livestock under the cover of darkness and sold them quickly for profit. He also helped himself to grain, gasoline, antiques, and anything else of value that wasn't securely locked up. If something went missing in the area, locals typically had a good idea of who was responsible, though few dared to say it aloud.

As he entered adulthood, McElroy's personal life was as chaotic as his professional one. He fathered more than ten children with multiple women and cycled through a series of marriages and relationships. His treatment of women was notoriously abusive, and he seemed to view them as possessions rather than partners. By the late 1970s, he was married to a young woman named Trena McCloud, whose relationship with McElroy had begun under particularly disturbing circumstances.

For more than twenty years, Ken McElroy operated with near impunity in and around Skidmore. The list of crimes attributed to him grew steadily more serious as time went on: assault, arson, statutory rape, child molestation, cattle rustling, burglary, and attempted murder. Yet despite being indicted twenty-one different times for various felonies,

McElroy managed to avoid conviction with remarkable consistency.

His success in evading justice stemmed from a two-pronged strategy. First, McElroy retained the services of Richard Gene McFadin, a skilled defense attorney from nearby Maryville who specialized in keeping troublesome clients out of jail. McFadin later described McElroy as the "best client I ever had," noting that he always paid in cash, showed up on time for appointments, and adamantly insisted on his innocence in every case.

McElroy and McFadin manipulated the legal system with surprising effectiveness, requesting continuances and delays that pushed court dates months or years into the future. When trials finally occurred, McFadin aggressively attacked witness credibility or produced surprise alibis that cast just enough doubt to secure acquittals.

The second and more sinister part of McElroy's strategy involved brutal intimidation. Anyone who testified against him quickly learned the consequences. McElroy parked his distinctive red pickup outside their homes for hours, sometimes with his shotgun visibly displayed. He followed them around town, making phone calls at odd hours or simply appearing wherever they went, ensuring they understood they were being watched.

The case of farmer Romaine Henry demonstrated McElroy's methods perfectly. In July 1976, Henry accused McElroy of shooting guns on his property. McElroy responded by shooting Henry twice with a shotgun, seriously wounding him. Although Henry survived and pressed charges, McElroy launched a campaign of terror against him. By Henry's own count, McElroy parked near his home over 100 times, sometimes firing shotgun blasts into the air at night—wordless reminders of what awaited Henry if he testified.

When the trial finally occurred, McElroy's lawyer produced two surprise witnesses claiming McElroy was hunting raccoons elsewhere during the shooting. McFadin also attacked Henry's character by dredging up a decades-old minor conviction. The result was another acquittal despite clear evidence.

This pattern repeated throughout Nodaway County. People who crossed McElroy, no matter how trivially, found themselves under siege until they backed down. The few who pressed charges often recanted or refused to cooperate by trial time, too frightened of the consequences for themselves and their families.

"He knew which people to pick on. The weak people. And he followed through on his threats just often enough to make people believe he was going to do what he said," observed one local resident.

By the late 1970s, Skidmore existed in a state of constant anxiety. McElroy's influence had grown so pervasive that many residents felt like prisoners in their own town. They adjusted their daily routines to avoid potential encounters with him. Parents instructed children to give McElroy a wide berth, farmers who suspected him of stealing often chose silence over confrontation, and many avoided certain roads or businesses if his truck was spotted nearby.

The psychological toll on the community was immense. Even local law enforcement felt the strain. Confronting McElroy meant potentially facing down a violent man who carried multiple firearms and had shown no hesitation about using them. For the citizens of Skidmore, there seemed to be no escape from the shadow McElroy cast over their lives.

Perhaps the most disturbing aspect of McElroy's reign of terror was his relationship with his wife, Trena. Their story began when Trena was just twelve years old, a child from a poor family in the area. McElroy, then in his forties, began sexually abusing the girl, eventually making her pregnant at age fourteen. When her parents tried to intervene, McElroy responded with characteristic brutality: He burned their house down and shot their dog, then threatened to kidnap their other daughter if they didn't allow him to take Trena.

Faced with such threats and feeling abandoned by authorities, Trena's parents reluctantly consented to her marriage with McElroy, essentially handing their daughter over to her abuser. It was a calculated move on McElroy's part—by marrying Trena, he avoided potential statutory rape charges since a wife generally couldn't be compelled to testify against her husband. The arrangement was a stark illustration of how completely McElroy had managed to circumvent both the law and basic human decency.

As the 1970s gave way to the 1980s, the situation in Skidmore reached a breaking point. The legal system had proven itself utterly incapable of stopping McElroy, and the town's collective frustration was building toward an inevitable explosion. That explosion would be triggered by a seemingly minor incident at a local grocery store.

In 1980, the Bowenkamp family ran the grocery store in Skidmore, one of the few remaining businesses on the town's main street. Seventy-year-old Ernest "Bo" Bowenkamp and his wife Lois were known for their fair dealings and willingness to extend credit to neighbors during hard times. The couple had lived in Skidmore for decades, raising their children there and serving as pillars of the community.

One day, a clerk at the store believed one of McElroy's young daughters—a child he had with Trena—had attempted to steal candy. The situation should have been a minor one, the kind of small-town incident typically resolved with a gentle reprimand and perhaps a call to the child's parents. Lois Bowenkamp spoke to the girl, later claiming she had tried to smooth things over. However, when Trena McElroy heard about what had happened, she told Ken that their daughter had been insulted and accused of theft.

Ken McElroy

For a man like McElroy, who viewed any slight as a personal affront requiring retribution, this trivial matter became the pretext for a campaign of harassment against the older couple. In a bizarre move, he initially offered Lois money to engage in a fistfight with Trena to settle the matter—an offer she naturally refused. Rebuffed and enraged, McElroy then began a systematic intimidation campaign against the Bowenkamps that would escalate over the following months.

Almost every night, McElroy parked his truck outside the Bowenkamp home or the grocery store after closing time. He sat there for hours, watching and sometimes firing his shotgun into the air to terrorize the family. The Bowenkamps reported feeling like prisoners, never knowing what McElroy might do next. Other townspeople looked on with growing alarm; many had suffered McElroy's intimidation before, but targeting an elderly couple over candy seemed extreme even for him.

On the evening of July 8, 1980, the situation finally boiled over into violence. Bo Bowenkamp was standing on the loading dock behind his grocery store, waiting for a repairman to arrive and fix an appliance. As dusk fell, McElroy drove up to the back of the store, armed with a shotgun. In a calculated move, he first bribed two local boys to go buy sodas at a nearby vending machine, perhaps to remove potential witnesses from the immediate area.

Then, without warning or provocation, McElroy raised his shotgun and fired at the elderly grocer. The blast hit Bowenkamp in the neck, sending him crashing to the ground in a pool of blood. As Bowenkamp lay grievously wounded, McElroy calmly fled the scene in his truck. Bo's wife and others rushed to his aid, and miraculously, despite the severe injury, he survived the attack.

The community was horrified. This was different from McElroy's previous crimes—he had nearly killed a beloved seventy-year-old store owner over what amounted to a piece of candy. The shooting of Bo Bowenkamp crossed a line that even the most fearful residents of Skidmore could not ignore.

Law enforcement responded swiftly. Missouri state troopers tracked down and arrested McElroy a few hours after the shooting. He was charged with attempted murder and other offenses in connection with the attack. For once, it seemed justice might be within reach. The case against McElroy was strong, with multiple eyewitnesses and clear evidence. Even his formidable lawyer, Richard McFadin, couldn't get him off the hook entirely.

At trial in 1981, a jury found McElroy guilty of the assault charge—but, shockingly, not the attempted murder charge. This was a distinction that infuriated townspeople who had seen the viciousness of the attack. The two-year prison sentence struck many as absurdly lenient for shooting a seventy-year-old man at point-blank range. Still, it represented the first real legal consequence McElroy had ever faced, and Skidmore's residents hoped their tormentor would finally be behind bars.

But their relief evaporated almost immediately. At that time in Missouri, defendants could remain free on bail while appealing their convictions. McElroy, true to form, exploited this loophole. He posted bond and walked out of court a free man on the very same day he was sentenced, mocking the system that had failed to contain him yet again.

What happened next would push the town of Skidmore beyond its breaking point.

On the afternoon of July 8, 1981, exactly one year after shooting Bo Bowenkamp, Ken McElroy celebrated his temporary freedom by visiting the D&G Tavern in downtown Skidmore. The D&G was one of the town's few gathering spots, a place where farmers and townspeople stopped for a drink after work. McElroy arrived at the tavern carrying a rifle with a bayonet attached—a blatant violation of the terms of his release, which prohibited him from possessing firearms.

As he walked inside, McElroy made no attempt to hide his weapon or his intentions. In a loud voice heard by everyone present, he bragged about how he planned to finish the job on Bo Bowenkamp, describing in graphic detail how he would kill him this time. The patrons listened in stunned silence as McElroy laid out his plans for murder, brazenly unconcerned about witnesses or consequences.

For many in the tavern that day, something finally snapped. They had watched McElroy intimidate, threaten, and harm their neighbors for decades. They had seen him escape justice time and again through legal maneuvering and witness intimidation. Now, fresh from a conviction that should have put him in prison, he was openly planning his next violent crime. If the justice system couldn't protect them from Ken McElroy, they realized, no one could.

Word of McElroy's threats spread quickly through Skidmore. Within hours, concerned citizens began discussing what, if anything, they could legally do to protect Bo Bowenkamp and the community at large. Someone suggested a town meeting to address the crisis, and plans were made to gather the following morning at the American Legion Hall in downtown Skidmore.

On the morning of July 10, 1981, approximately sixty Skidmore residents assembled at the Legion Hall. Among them were the Bowenkamps and their family, local business owners, farmers, and ordinary citizens who had endured years of McElroy's terrorism. Also present was Nodaway County Sheriff Dan Estes, who had agreed to speak with the townspeople about their options.

The atmosphere in the hall was tense and emotional. People openly voiced their fears and frustrations, sharing stories of how McElroy had harassed or harmed them over the years. The central question on everyone's mind was straightforward: How could they protect themselves and their community from a man who seemed immune to legal consequences?

Sheriff Estes urged restraint. Aware of how volatile the situation had become, he recommended forming a neighborhood watch or community alert system to monitor McElroy's movements. His message was clear: Let the legal system work, and don't take matters into your own hands. However, many in the crowd felt this approach was woefully inadequate—essentially just more waiting and watching while McElroy plotted further violence.

Shortly after conveying this message, Sheriff Estes left the meeting to attend to other business outside of town. His departure meant no law enforcement presence remained in Skidmore that morning. Some later speculated that Estes had deliberately removed himself, perhaps sensing what might transpire and not wanting to witness it.

As the meeting continued, a breathless resident burst through the door with urgent news: Ken McElroy and Trena had just arrived in town and were currently sitting at the D&G Tavern, barely a block away. It was approaching noon, and McElroy was apparently following his usual routine of coming into Skidmore for a midday drink, seemingly oblivious to the charged atmosphere.

When this news reached the assembled townspeople, a collective resolve seemed to form. Without explicit planning or discussion, people began filing out of the Legion Hall and walking down Main Street toward the tavern. Some entered the tavern, while others remained outside, creating an unusual concentration of people on the typically quiet street.

Inside the D&G Tavern, McElroy sat nursing a drink with Trena beside him, suddenly surrounded by an unusually large number of townspeople. The atmosphere was thick with tension, but no confrontation took place inside the building. McElroy may have sensed the hostility, but he maintained his composure, buying a six-pack of beer to go and paying for cigarettes before standing up to leave.

As McElroy walked out of the tavern with Trena close by his side, a crowd followed them onto the main street. The time was approximately 11:30 a.m. on a bright summer day. McElroy and Trena climbed into his red Chevy pickup truck, which was parked on the street. The crowd of men and women—estimates range from thirty to forty-six people—stood in clusters nearby, watching intently as McElroy settled into the driver's seat, placed his beer on the dashboard, lit a cigarette, and put the key in the ignition. And then the silence was shattered.

Multiple gunshots suddenly erupted in the quiet midday air. More than twenty rounds were fired in quick succession from at least two different directions—one from behind McElroy's truck, another from down the street in front of it. Some bystanders instinctively dropped to the ground for cover. Trena, sitting beside her husband, ducked down and began screaming as bullets hit the vehicle.

Ken McElroy was struck by at least two bullets almost simultaneously. One was a heavy caliber round that smashed through the back window of the pickup, while another, smaller caliber bullet hit him from a different angle. Both rounds found their mark in McElroy's head and neck, inflicting catastrophic injuries. The shots were believed to have come from a high-powered rifle and a smaller twenty-two-caliber weapon.

McElroy slumped over the steering wheel, killed instantly or within moments by the severe wounds. Glass from the truck's windows scattered across the street, and the pickup's body was left peppered with bullet holes. The engine was still running, with McElroy's foot on the brake pedal.

The gunfire ceased as abruptly as it had begun. When the echoes faded, McElroy lay motionless in the driver's seat, bleeding from his head wounds. Trena managed to climb out of the truck, screaming hysterically and covered in her husband's blood. A man from the crowd gently took her by the arm and led her away from the gruesome scene.

In the immediate aftermath, an eerie calm fell over the street. No one called for an ambulance. No one rushed to McElroy's aid. The townspeople began to disperse quietly, many heading to their cars or back to their farms. Others lingered as if in shock. When Sheriff Estes returned to Skidmore after hearing reports of gunfire, he found McElroy's body, a distraught Trena, and dozens of shell-shocked residents—but no one claimed to have seen who fired the shots.

Investigators tried to piece together what had happened in broad daylight on Main Street. They questioned those still at the scene, asking who had fired the shots. The response, repeated over and over, was some variation of "I didn't see anything." Some claimed they ducked for cover when the shooting started. Others said they thought it was firecrackers at first and didn't catch a glimpse of the gunmen.

Only Trena McElroy provided a name. Through her tears and shock, she accused a local farmer named Del Clement of being one of the shooters, claiming he had been standing behind the truck. However, no one from the crowd corroborated her account. Clement himself never admitted involvement and was never formally charged. Apart from Trena's accusation, the wall of silence from the townspeople was nearly unanimous.

Sheriff Estes and other investigators were faced with an extraordinary situation: A murder had been committed in front of dozens of witnesses in broad daylight, yet no one was willing to identify the perpetrators. It was as if an unspoken agreement had instantly formed among the citizens of Skidmore—they would protect whoever had pulled the triggers, maintaining a code of silence that would prove impossible to break.

In the days and weeks following McElroy's death, law enforcement officials mounted an intensive investigation. The Nodaway County Prosecutor's Office, the Missouri Highway Patrol, and even the FBI were involved, given the unusual circumstances. Over one hundred interviews were conducted with residents of Skidmore and the surrounding area. Agents went door to door, asking the same questions over and over, but the results were always the same: No one saw the shooters.

The collective denial was not orchestrated in any formal way; it seemed to arise organically from a shared understanding among Skidmore's citizens. They all knew what had happened and, in many cases, likely knew who was responsible. But they considered McElroy's death a form of community justice—a fate he had brought upon himself. The attitude of many townspeople was simply that "he needed killing."

This blanket silence thwarted any attempt to build a criminal case. Without cooperative witnesses, prosecutors knew they couldn't convince a jury beyond a reasonable doubt that any specific individual had committed the crime. Eventually, both a county grand jury and a federal grand jury declined to issue any indictments. The case stalled and was eventually closed, officially leaving Ken McElroy's death unsolved.

In Skidmore, there was no appetite for second-guessing what had happened. To the townspeople, justice had been served on July 10, 1981, even if by their own hands. Many residents adopted a "don't ask, don't tell" policy. They simply didn't discuss the shooting—not with outsiders, and often not even with each other. This silence was so pervasive that it attracted national media attention. Reporters who came to Skidmore looking for answers found a community closed in on itself, with no one willing to talk about who had fired the fatal shots.

One of the few people to speak publicly was Cheryl Huston, daughter of Bo Bowenkamp. She said the town saw

McElroy's death as justice for everything he had put them through, and once the decision was made to stay silent, no one broke ranks. Investigators could have questioned them endlessly and still come up empty. In the end, no one was ever arrested for the killing.

The only legal repercussion came in the form of a civil lawsuit. In July 1984, nearly three years after the shooting, Trena McElroy filed a wrongful death suit against multiple defendants: the Town of Skidmore, Nodaway County, Sheriff Dan Estes, and Del Clement, the man she had accused of firing the shots. However, the suit was settled out of court in 1985 for $17,600—a relatively small sum—with no party admitting guilt or liability.

With McElroy gone, the town of Skidmore experienced a profound transformation. For the first time in years, people slept soundly, no longer jumping at every creak or distant engine sound. Bo and Lois Bowenkamp could live their remaining years in peace, farmers no longer posted overnight guards for their livestock, and parents allowed their children to roam the neighborhood freely. One resident summed up the collective mood, saying, "It was like we could all breathe again."

Yet the killing left a complex legacy. Skidmore now carried a new burden: a reputation as the town that got away with murder. National media portrayed it as a vigilante community that had taken Old West-style justice into the modern era. This image persisted for decades, with articles and television news programs revisiting the case on major anniversaries, bringing unwanted attention to a community that simply wanted to move on.

For those directly involved in the case, life continued in various ways. Del Clement remained in the area until his death in 2009. He never confessed or was charged in connection with the shooting. Trena McElroy remarried and moved to Lebanon, Missouri, where she lived until her death from cancer in 2012 at the age of fifty-five. McElroy's defense attorney, Richard McFadin, continued his legal practice and occasionally spoke about his infamous client and the town that got away with murder.

The D&G Tavern eventually closed its doors. By the early 2000s, it was an empty shell—a hollow reminder of that fateful day. David Baird, the young prosecutor who had been newly appointed just before McElroy's killing, retired decades later with the case still technically open and unsolved. His successor opted not to reopen the long-dormant investigation, acknowledging that the trail was cold and the town's code of silence was unbreakable.

Even members of law enforcement, in quieter moments, seemed to accept the outcome. Richard Stratton, a retired Missouri Highway Patrol trooper who had been involved in the case, reflected years later on why the townspeople acted as they did: "Those were fathers and grandfathers on the street in Skidmore that day. Ordinary, hardworking people. They did what they did because we didn't do our job. Then they went home and kept their mouths shut."

This was a remarkable admission from a law officer: an understanding that the community felt compelled to deliver justice on their own because the legal system had failed to protect them. The county sheriff at the time of the shooting, Danny Estes, was similarly philosophical about the outcome. While he never condoned what happened, he acknowledged the systemic failures that led to it. "McElroy had terrorized that town for twenty years," Estes said years later. "He'd been charged twenty-one times and never once convicted. Tell me that isn't justice denied."

The Ken McElroy case remains one of the most widely recognized acts of vigilante justice in American history—unsolved on paper, though few believe the truth is unknown. His killing ended a reign of terror and ushered in a long-standing silence that has endured for more than four decades. It was, in every sense, a perfect crime: everybody saw it, and nobody saw it.

CHAPTER 12
THE MILLIONAIRE

Built in the picturesque English countryside of Shropshire, Osbaston House stood as a proud symbol of wealth and achievement. The imposing three-story mansion and its manicured grounds represented everything its owner, Christopher Foster, had worked for: success, status, and the security of a life removed from his humble beginnings. The fifteen-acre estate, with its stables, outbuildings, and sprawling gardens, was the perfect family retreat, isolated enough to provide privacy yet grand enough to impress visitors.

On the mild summer evening of August 25, 2008, neighbors would recall seeing the lights of Osbaston House glowing warmly against the darkening sky. Inside, life appeared to be continuing as normal for the Foster family. Christopher, his wife Jill, and their fifteen-year-old daughter Kirstie had returned from a neighbor's barbecue earlier that evening, where they had seemed relaxed and in good spirits. None of the party guests would later recall anything unusual about the family's behavior that day. Christopher had enjoyed the afternoon shooting clay pigeons, drinking with friends, and putting on the confident face of a successful businessman.

But behind that carefully maintained façade, Christopher Foster's world was collapsing. Unknown to most in his social circle, the millionaire businessman was just hours away from an act of destruction so complete, so meticulously executed, that investigators would later describe it as "cold and clinical"—almost like a military operation.

By sunrise the next morning, Osbaston House would be transformed into a smoldering ruin, the site of a tragedy that would shock Britain and leave a community searching for answers amid the ashes.

At fifty years old, Christopher Foster had the trappings of a self-made man. Born into modest circumstances in the West Midlands, he had risen through ambition and a knack for spotting business opportunities. His breakthrough came in the late 1990s, when he developed a specialized type of insulation for oil rigs that earned the highest fire safety rating possible. The product, UlvaShield, became the cornerstone of his company, Ulva Ltd, which he founded in 1998.

Business boomed quickly. By 1999, Foster had secured a £500,000 export deal for an offshore rig in Canada and was reporting an annual turnover of £1.5 million—a figure he claimed would double the following year. The money rolled in faster than Foster had ever imagined. With newfound wealth came the lifestyle he had always craved: the country mansion purchased for over £1 million and luxury cars including two Porsches, an Aston Martin, and a Range Rover. He even bought a tractor for his sprawling property, embracing the role of country gentleman with enthusiasm.

To those on the outside, Foster was living the dream. He kept horses on his estate for his equestrian-loving wife and daughter, his charisma and cash gave him social confidence, and the Foster family was often the envy of their social circle. However, Foster's spending far outpaced any long-term planning, a fact that would later prove catastrophic. An accountant who worked with him noted that Foster lived for immediate indulgence, focused on "What can I do now?" rather than preparing for the future.

This wasn't the only crack in Foster's seemingly perfect life. Behind the scenes, he maintained a string of extramarital affairs—at least eight mistresses, according to his sister-in-law. His wife, Jill, quietly tolerated these indiscretions, maintaining the outward appearance of a happy, wealthy family.

By the mid-2000s, the business empire that fueled Foster's extravagant lifestyle began to crumble. Financial records showed that by 2005, Ulva Ltd's liabilities exceeded its assets by approximately £2.8 million. The company was hemorrhaging money, largely due to Foster's lavish personal spending on homes, cars, guns, and exclusive memberships.

Desperately trying to cut costs, Foster breached an exclusive supply contract with a distributor, DRC Distribution Ltd, by sourcing materials elsewhere. This led to a legal battle that would accelerate his downfall. In July 2007, the High Court ruled that Ulva Ltd had indeed breached its contract, leaving DRC with an £800,000 damages claim.

Rather than accept the judgment, Foster attempted to evade payment through corporate maneuvers. He formed a new holding company and transferred Ulva Ltd's business to it, then put the original company into administration to dodge creditors. When the case went to the Court of Appeal in February 2008, a judge condemned Foster's conduct as "an asset stripping exercise" and described him as "bereft of the basic instincts of commercial morality...not to be trusted."

By late 2007, Ulva Ltd had entered compulsory liquidation, and the Foster family's finances were in disarray. Court orders had effectively tied up Osbaston House, prohibiting its sale without approval and ultimately transferring control to insolvency practitioners handling Ulva's collapse.

The extent of Foster's debt was staggering—approximately £2 million, including £1 million to DRC and £800,000 to the UK tax authority. Creditors were moving to repossess his beloved family home, the symbol of everything he had achieved. By the summer of 2008, Foster had lost his company, his patented invention had been seized, and he faced losing the lifestyle to which he and his family had grown accustomed.

The pressure was crushing him. Foster confided to a friend that Jill and Kirstie were accustomed to luxury and "would not be able to cope" with losing it. He hinted at external blame for his troubles, telling two friends he was owed millions by "Russians"—a claim that may have been more excuse than reality. His mental health deteriorated rapidly, and he told his doctor about suicidal thoughts and despair over his situation.

What made this situation even more dangerous was that despite his suicidal ideation, Foster possessed firearms—he was a licensed gun owner and avid shooter. The red flags were there, but the disconnect between his mental health care and firearms licensing meant that authorities were never alerted to the potential danger.

Bank Holiday Monday, August 25, 2008, began as a pleasant day for the Foster family. They attended a barbecue at a neighbor's house in their rural Shropshire community, which included an informal clay pigeon shoot—one of Christopher's favorite pastimes.

Witnesses later recounted that the family—Chris, Jill, and Kirstie—"all seemed completely normal" that afternoon and evening. Christopher, in particular, appeared jovial: He participated in the shooting and drank alcohol with friends. One guest noted that Chris became somewhat intoxicated by the end of the gathering, but nothing about his behavior raised concerns.

The Fosters were among the last to leave the barbecue, departing around 8:30 p.m. that evening, thanking their hosts, and heading back to Osbaston House, just a short drive away. No one at the party could have possibly imagined that within hours, Christopher Foster would enact a plan to erase his family and destroy everything he had built.

As darkness fell on August 25, Christopher set in motion a premeditated plan to annihilate everything he viewed as threatened by his failure—his wife, his child, his home, his animals, and himself.

In the dark early hours of Tuesday, August 26, 2008, Christopher Foster carried out a horrifying sequence of events at his estate. Sometime after midnight, as forty-nine-year-old Jill and fifteen-year-old Kirstie slept, Foster retrieved his twenty-two-caliber rifle, a weapon he legally owned. He had outfitted the rifle with a silencer, ensuring the gunshots would not be heard by neighbors—or possibly even by other occupants in the large house.

Moving quietly through the darkened rooms, Christopher first shot his wife in the back of the head at close range while she lay in bed, killing her instantly. He then went to Kirstie's room and shot his teenage daughter in the head as well. Forensic pathologists later determined that Kirstie died from a head wound consistent with a gunshot.

The shots were muffled by the silencer and the house's thick walls. Neither woman showed signs of struggle or awareness of the impending attack. It was a swift execution, carried out with an almost clinical efficiency.

With his family now lifeless in their beds, Christopher turned to the family's animals. Around 3:00 a.m., he began systematically killing the household pets. The Fosters had four dogs and several horses in their stables. Security footage from the estate's CCTV system captured Foster moving about outside, with two of the family's dogs following him across the courtyard. This was the last time those dogs were seen alive. Moments later, the CCTV showed Foster carrying what appeared to be the dead bodies of the dogs toward the stables.

Christopher Foster

Next, Foster went to the stable block and shot the three horses as they stood in their stalls. He wasn't just destroying his family; he was methodically eliminating every living creature in his care.

Having murdered his family and pets, Christopher moved to seal off the property and set it ablaze. The CCTV cameras recorded him driving a horsebox trailer down his long driveway and positioning it sideways across the main gate to block the estate's entrance. He then shot out its tires to ensure it couldn't be moved, effectively creating a barricade to prevent fire engines or anyone else from reaching the house.

Over the next thirty minutes, Foster methodically spread flammable materials and ignited multiple fires. Security footage showed him carrying his rifle over his shoulder with what investigators believed to be a battery pack on his belt. He also carried a bucket and plastic piping.

Foster had engineered a way to use the property's heating fuel as an accelerant. He cut a hole in the 2,000-liter diesel heating oil tank outside the house and attached a hose leading into the house's boiler room near the kitchen, creating an oil pipeline to flood the interiors with flammable fuel.

Inside the mansion, Foster had already staged additional accelerants. In the ground-floor library, he placed a metal drum filled with flammable liquid on its side and laid out towels soaked in fuel across the floor.

At approximately 3:45 a.m., the CCTV recorded a flash of light near the stables as Foster ignited a fire. Almost immediately, a powerful explosion erupted—likely the first drum of fuel going up in flames. This explosion disturbed the family's flock of doves and sent smoke billowing into the night sky. The stable block was soon engulfed in fire, and flames tore through the garage and outbuildings.

After starting the fires outside, Christopher returned to the mansion to finish his grim task. He likely ignited the prepared accelerants in the library, and very quickly, the ground floor was consumed by flames that spread to the upper floors.

Foster didn't attempt to flee. With the house burning around him, he positioned himself in the master bedroom suite where Jill's body lay. He lay down beside his wife's lifeless body on the floor as the toxic smoke and fire closed in. He still had his rifle with him, but he did not use the gun on himself. Instead, he chose to die by smoke inhalation.

Within minutes, the once-opulent mansion was transformed into an inferno, with flames bursting from windows and the roof and heavy smoke visible for miles.

Around 4:00 a.m., neighbors noticed the fire and called emergency services. Firefighters from Shropshire Fire and Rescue Service arrived to confront a towering blaze consuming Osbaston House. They were immediately impeded by the horsebox barricading the front gates, which made it impossible to drive fire engines up the long driveway.

Precious minutes were lost as crews tried to find another way in. When they finally approached the house, the heat was overwhelming. The roof had already collapsed in places, and firefighters were forced to keep a safe distance as jet streams of water were directed from afar into the inferno.

By dawn, Osbaston House was nothing more than a smoldering ruin—the skeletal brick walls were blackened, and the interior was reduced to ash. In the courtyard, the burnt-out frames of vehicles could be seen, including Christopher's Range Rover (with the personalized plate "JILL 40" that he had gifted Jill for her fortieth birthday) and one of his Porsches.

The firefighters didn't know it yet, but inside the burning house lay the bodies of Jill, Kirstie, and Christopher Foster.

At daybreak, firefighters and police faced a challenging scene. The fire was eventually extinguished after several hours, leaving unstable heaps of debris. One fire officer observed a hole cut into the heating oil tank with a pipe leading out—a clear indication that the fire had been intentionally set and fed with fuel. This was now a crime scene, not just a fire scene.

West Mercia Police opened an investigation, initially treating the Fosters as missing persons who might be victims. There was early speculation in the community—some wondered if the family had been kidnapped or if an outsider was involved. Police even put ports and airports on alert in case Christopher Foster or a suspect tried to flee the country.

Due to the structural wreckage, it took investigators time to safely enter and search the ruins. Structural engineers had to shore up parts of the house before search teams could sift through tons of debris by hand, looking for human remains and clues.

On August 27, as the rubble cooled, police confirmed the discovery of the remains of the three horses. This was a tell-tale sign; a random arsonist would have little reason to shoot the horses, suggesting an insider's deliberate act. Investigators also recovered spent and unspent firearm cartridges scattered around the property.

By August 30, search teams made a crucial find: two bodies in the main part of the house, the remains in poor condition due to the extreme heat. They were found near each other on the ground floor beneath what had been the master bedroom area. A twenty-two-caliber rifle was recovered lying near the bodies.

A forensic examination confirmed that it was Christopher's legally owned rifle. On August 31, dental records positively identified one body as forty-nine-year-old Jill Foster. The other was presumed to be Christopher. A post-mortem on Jill left no doubt as to the cause of death: She had died from a gunshot wound to the head prior to the fire.

It took until September 1 for searchers to locate the third body, that of young Kirstie. Her remains were found beneath collapsed debris in what had been her bedroom. Once retrieved, they were forensically identified as Kirstie.

Detective Superintendent Jon Groves, the lead investigator, summarized their conclusions: "We believe that Mr. Foster killed his wife and daughter before setting the fires which destroyed his home... We believe he then took his own life after setting the house alight."

The evidence was overwhelming. CCTV footage from the property showed Christopher Foster carrying a rifle and behaving in an "unhurried, deliberate" manner as the outbuildings burst into flames. In that footage, Foster is seen blocking the gates with the horsebox and firing a rifle at its tires.

Ballistic tests on the recovered rifle linked it to the shootings, and forensic analysts confirmed the elaborate arson setup. All the family's pets were found shot dead, and the front door had been barricaded from within.

The autopsy confirmed that Christopher Foster had died from smoke inhalation—there was no self-inflicted gunshot wound. Toxicology tests also revealed alcohol in his system, showing he had been drinking the night he carried out the murders.

What drove Christopher Foster to such extreme actions? The motive appears to be a combination of financial ruin, wounded pride, and a warped sense of "saving" his loved ones from a life he deemed unworthy.

It was the endgame of a man making a desperate attempt to avoid financial ruin and public humiliation. Facing bankruptcy and eviction, Foster likely saw annihilation as preferable to the shame of failure. He had told a friend that his family wouldn't cope with a backward step in lifestyle, suggesting he rationalized that killing them was better than letting them live in relative poverty or witness his disgrace.

Those who knew the Fosters struggled to reconcile the image of the devoted father with the man who murdered his family. Kirstie's headteacher said Foster had doted on his daughter.

Foster's psychological state in 2008 was fragile and depressed. He had taken steps that indicated suicidal tendencies and had told his doctor he felt like "doing himself in." The coroner's inquest revealed that he had been clinically mentally ill leading up to the event.

Pride and ego also played significant roles. Journalist Jon Ronson, who investigated the case, theorized that Foster's acts had an element of an "honor killing" of sorts—not in the cultural sense, but in that Christopher was too ashamed to face his family with his failures. He shot Jill and Kirstie in the back of the head, which Ronson interpreted as Foster being "too ashamed to look at them" as he killed them.

In his twisted logic, wiping out the family could have been his way of preserving their honor; they'd never live as the family of a disgraced man, simultaneously ending their suffering before it began. It's a pattern seen in other cases of men who kill families due to financial stress—an overidentification with one's role as a provider and an inability to accept any other outcome.

Foster also exhibited narcissistic traits. His past behavior—fraudulent business dealings, multiple affairs, and lavish excess—suggested a man focused on image and accustomed to getting his way. When the façade crumbled, rather than accept help or declare bankruptcy, he chose to erase the life he had built.

His mother perhaps encapsulated the motive best: "They were a very close, loving family unit, and I don't think he could face telling them they were going to lose everything." She added, "I can't condone what he's done," but "I've lost a dearly loved son, daughter-in-law, and beautiful granddaughter." Enid admitted the financial collapse came as a tremendous shock to the family, as Christopher had confided in nobody about it.

The motive can be seen as a toxic mix of financial desperation, fear of humiliation, distorted love, and mental illness. Foster's actions fit a narrative seen in similar cases: A middle-aged man with a history of control and success who can't countenance the loss of status and, instead of letting his family experience downward mobility or pity, decides to kill them and often himself, sometimes referred to as "extended suicide."

The coroner's investigation highlighted a crucial failure: Foster had told his GP he felt suicidal, yet this did not trigger any alert to authorities who had granted him a firearms license. In his recommendations, the coroner urged that medical professionals and firearms licensing authorities should share information in the future.

From the family's perspective, reactions were of profound grief and bewilderment. Jill's relatives were devastated; her sister, Ann Giddings, spoke about how Jill had tried to keep the family together despite Christopher's flaws, mentioning the affairs and how Jill played the dutiful wife.

Animal lovers were also appalled to learn that Foster had killed pets and horses. Some letters to the editor expressed outrage that he took innocent animals' lives. However, others saw it as further evidence of his mental disturbance.

The case of Christopher Foster stands as a devastating narrative of financial downfall turning into familial destruction. In a matter of hours, a man who once appeared to have it all—wealth, a loving family, and an estate—extinguished the lives of his wife and daughter, slaughtered his pets, and destroyed every physical trace of their affluent life before taking his own.

CHAPTER 13
A FAMILIAR FACE

The winter sun was already beginning its early descent as six-year-old Randy Brown left Woodlawn Elementary School on Monday, January 26, 1976. The first-grader bundled his coat against the cool Texas Gulf breeze as he began his journey home—a route he had walked many times before through the streets of Corpus Christi. Randy was known by teachers as a "bashful and shy" boy, "not one to go with strangers." Standing at just over three feet tall with dark hair and bright eyes, the young boy was recognizable to most in the close-knit neighborhood.

What happened next would forever shatter this community.

As Randy turned onto Beatrice Street, roughly two blocks north of his school, a familiar figure approached him. Justin Bradley Fox, twenty-two, lived nearby and was a face every child knew. Fox often played with the local children, and parents thought nothing of it—he seemed harmless, if a bit immature.

It was this false sense of security that would prove fatal.

Fox convinced Randy to come with him, a task made easier by the fact that Fox wasn't a stranger at all. Several neighbors later recalled seeing the first-grader walking alongside the young man on the bicycle, an image that would later haunt them. What nobody could have known was that Randy Brown would never make it home that day. By morning, his name would be front-page news in a case that would shock the coastal Texas community to its core.

Randy's parents became increasingly concerned when he failed to arrive home from school that afternoon. A call to neighbors confirmed their worst fears—their son was missing. Time was slipping away with each passing moment.

The Browns immediately alerted police and organized a search. Within hours, scores of friends, neighbors, and even citizen band radio owners had fanned out across South Corpus Christi, desperately searching for the missing boy.

Radio calls crackled between volunteer searchers as they methodically combed the residential areas near Woodlawn Elementary. Police joined the effort, knocking on doors and questioning anyone who might have seen the child. Hope remained that Randy had perhaps visited a friend or gotten lost.

"We thought possibly he might have gone to a friend's house, but as searches continued, we became more and more concerned and the police became more and more concentrated in their search," said a family friend who helped coordinate the volunteer effort.

The search for Randy continued into the night. As darkness fell, the anxiety among searchers grew palpable. Many hoped for a happy resolution, but as the hours passed, a sense of dread began to settle over the neighborhood.

Police Lieutenant C.L. Wimbish had been coordinating officers in the search for Randy since the first alert went out. At approximately 11:30 p.m., nearly eight hours after Randy had disappeared, a discovery was made that would transform the missing person case into something far more sinister.

It was just before midnight when Justin Fox's stepmother made a gruesome discovery at their home on Rickey Street, only four blocks from Randy's usual route home. While moving through the house, she noticed something that made her blood run cold—what appeared to be a small leg protruding from beneath her stepson's bed.

Pulling back the bedding, she uncovered the nude body of a small child. In shock, she immediately contacted the authorities.

Police arrived within minutes. Randy Brown's body was found partly hidden beneath Justin's bed, carefully concealed but for the small leg that gave away the grim secret. Medical personnel at the scene confirmed the boy was deceased.

Later, an autopsy would reveal the horrifying details: Randy had been strangled to death and sexually assaulted. According to the medical examiner, the child had likely been dead for approximately eight hours before his body was discovered, placing the time of death shortly after his abduction.

The news hit the tight-knit community like a physical blow. Parents clutched their children closer, neighbors locked doors that had previously remained open, and an overwhelming sense of disbelief settled over Corpus Christi. How could something so heinous happen in their community, at the hands of someone who had lived among them?

Police quickly issued an all-points bulletin for Justin Bradley Fox. He was located and arrested just hours later, around 1:30 a.m. on January 27, at a relative's home. Fox was taken into custody without incident and transported to the Nueces County Jail, where he was charged with capital murder and kidnapping.

Justin Bradley Fox didn't fit the stereotype of a cold-blooded killer. Standing at an average height with dark hair and glasses, Fox was described by those who knew him as quiet and somewhat awkward. At twenty-two, he was unemployed and living with his family. His prior work experience included stints as a grocery store sacker, but nothing in his minimal employment history suggested any red flags.

Yet beneath this ordinary façade lurked something far more sinister.

Neighbors recalled Justin Fox as a "lonely boy" who often sought companionship with younger children in the area. One woman who lived nearby noted, "He played with the kids in the neighborhood. He would get down on his hands and knees, and he would play horsey with them. He roughhoused with the kids, but he never hurt them."

Those who had known Fox for years recalled a troubling shift in his behavior during his teens. According to several neighbors, he had been involved in a serious car accident that they believed had left him mentally affected. After the crash, they said, Fox was never quite the same—he withdrew socially and became noticeably more reclusive.

A former roommate from a summer camp four years prior described him as emotionally immature. "We knew Bradley needed greater self-confidence," the roommate recalled. "His emotional immaturity may have led him to seek companionship with younger people than himself."

Despite his unsettling behavior, Fox had no significant criminal record prior to Randy's murder. In fact, he was known to attend church regularly and had even distributed religious literature in the neighborhood shortly before the crime. Just days before Randy's murder, Fox had handed out church pamphlets to several homes in the area, presenting himself as a devout young man.

This double life—the churchgoing young adult who played innocently with neighborhood children versus the predator who would commit an unthinkable crime—left those who knew him reeling in confusion and disgust.

The case against Justin Bradley Fox was substantial from the beginning. Randy's body had been found in Fox's bedroom, and multiple witnesses had seen the boy with Fox shortly before his disappearance. Fox's own family members had discovered the crime and alerted authorities.

After his arrest, Fox gave a statement to police. While the full details of Fox's confession were never released to the public, investigators confirmed he admitted to his involvement. The physical evidence collected at the scene, combined with the autopsy findings and witness accounts, painted a disturbing picture of what had occurred. Investigators reconstructed that Randy had been abducted while walking home, taken to Fox's residence, sexually assaulted, and strangled to death.

The Assistant District Attorney took charge of the State's case against Fox. Given the heinous nature of the crime, prosecutors initially announced they would seek the death penalty. "In a case this serious, involving the murder, kidnapping, and sexual assault of a child, the state has no choice but to pursue the maximum penalty allowed by law," the prosecutor stated.

Fox's family retained an attorney for his defense. From the outset, the defense attorney requested a change of venue, concerned that the extensive pre-trial publicity would make it impossible for Fox to receive a fair trial in Corpus Christi. The prosecutor contested this motion, famously remarking to the press, "If Patty Hearst can be tried in San Francisco and Charles Manson in Los Angeles, then Justin Fox can be tried in Corpus Christi."

As the legal proceedings progressed, Fox underwent court-ordered psychological evaluations. The findings would later play a significant role in his defense strategy. Psychiatrists determined that Fox was intellectually below average—a "dullard," in their clinical assessment, indicating borderline intellectual functioning. Despite this diminished intellect, they found that Fox understood the difference between right and wrong, meaning an insanity defense would be unlikely to succeed.

As the legal machinery ground forward, the community of Corpus Christi grappled with the aftermath of Randy's murder. Schools implemented new safety measures, and a collective sense of innocence had been shattered.

At Woodlawn Elementary, where Randy had been a student, the administration took immediate steps to protect their pupils. The principal met with a group of concerned parents from the PTA and Woodlawn Community Advisory Committee to develop a comprehensive safety plan.

One of the initiatives was a "block mothers" program, where volunteers would place a sign in their window identifying their home as a safe haven for children in trouble. The school also planned an assembly to remind students about stranger danger—though in cruel irony, Justin Fox had not been a stranger to the children in the neighborhood. Additional measures included a new policy of verifying school absences by calling parents directly, a time-consuming but necessary precaution.

"They're all too young to realize what death is," said the school secretary, reflecting on how the students were processing the tragedy. "One little boy came in and asked if Randy got well."

For months after Randy's body was discovered, more parents than usual brought their children to school and picked them up afterward, unwilling to let them walk alone. The Brown family's grief was unimaginable. A day-long wake was held at their home, with religious overtones providing what comfort they could find. Randy was buried at Seaside Memorial Park after a moving service, where the family's pastor announced plans for a memorial fund in the boy's name.

As 1976 wore on, the city of Corpus Christi waited with bated breath for justice. The case against Justin Bradley Fox moved toward trial, with the evidence mounting like a dark storm cloud over the defendant's fate.

The proof was overwhelming. Several witnesses, the location of the body, and the physical evidence collected at the scene all pointed toward guilt. The autopsy findings confirming strangulation and sexual assault further strengthened the prosecution's case.

As jury selection was underway in November 1976, a dramatic turn of events occurred: Fox's defense team and the prosecution reached a plea agreement. In exchange for a guilty plea to the lesser included offense of murder, rather than capital murder, the State would withdraw its pursuit of the death penalty. This meant Fox would receive a life sentence instead of potentially facing execution.

What should have been a straightforward plea hearing on November 9, 1976, nearly collapsed when Fox hesitated during the judge's questioning. Asked if he understood what he was doing when he killed Randy, Fox claimed he was "not in my right mind at the time." This unexpected response threatened the plea agreement by calling into question Fox's legal sanity.

The courtroom held its collective breath as the proceedings paused while Fox consulted with his attorneys. When the court resumed, Fox changed course entirely. Questioned again if he knew what he was doing that January day and whether he knew it was wrong, Fox answered affirmatively to both. With these crucial admissions secured, the judge accepted his guilty plea to murder.

On December 1, 1976, a Nueces County jury formally found Justin Fox guilty of Randy Brown's murder. Even with Fox's guilty plea, Texas law at the time required a jury verdict on the issue of guilt. The punishment was fixed at life imprisonment, which was the mandatory sentence under the plea agreement.

During the sentencing phase, psychological testimony offered insights into Fox's state of mind. Fox's defense attorney reminded the court that "a life sentence in the penitentiary is not a great bargain" for a twenty-two-year-old man. A psychologist who had evaluated Fox claimed the young man "had effectively pronounced sentence on himself on the afternoon of January 26, 1976," by committing such a heinous crime.

The psychologist further testified that Fox exhibited emotional immaturity and loneliness but was not psychotic. In a statement that would prove hauntingly ironic, the expert opined that Fox was more inclined to hurt himself than anyone else.

Prosecutors, however, emphasized the brutality of the murder. They argued that for Fox, abusing and killing Randy had become "a compulsion" that he was unable to control—but that compulsion was no excuse for murder. The prosecution maintained that Fox was fully responsible for the heinous and unspeakable act against an innocent child and deserved a life term.

On January 3, 1977, Justin Bradley Fox appeared for the final time in District Court for formal sentencing. The judge confirmed the jury's verdict and imposed a life sentence. When asked if he had anything to say before sentencing, Fox replied with a simple, "No, sir."

After the trial concluded and Fox began serving his life sentence, the Corpus Christi community worked to ensure Randy Brown would not be forgotten. In April 1978, more than two years after the murder, the Gateway Christian Center in Corpus Christi dedicated the "Randy Brown Memorial Children's Chapel" in his honor. Family, friends, and neighbors gathered for the ceremony, ensuring that Randy's memory would live on in a positive way.

"We lost a son, but I have great sympathy for Fox's parents—they lost a son, too," Mrs. Brown told reporters at the chapel dedication. "We feel no bitterness." Despite this remarkable display of forgiveness, the Browns continued to struggle with their loss.

The chapel, which cost approximately $16,000 to build, was dedicated debt-free, with about $3,000 of the total cost donated by friends and neighbors of the Brown family. At the dedication ceremony, a pastor offered a sermon, and the Mayor cut the ribbon, officially opening the memorial space.

As for Justin Bradley Fox, his life sentence in the Texas Department of Corrections meant he would spend decades behind bars. A life sentence in Texas in the 1970s technically allowed for the possibility of parole after serving a minimum term, typically twenty years for capital cases. However, given the severity of Fox's crime—the abduction, sexual assault, and murder of a child—it's likely he would have faced significant challenges in any parole hearing.

Fox filed no appeals of his conviction or sentence. His case concluded at the trial court level in 1977, with the life term standing as final. His quiet acceptance of his punishment—a stark contrast to the brazen nature of his crime—brought a measure of closure to a community that had been deeply wounded by his actions.

In the end, Randy Brown's legacy lived on not in the darkness of his final moments but in the light of a community's determination to protect its children and honor his memory. The chapel dedicated in his name stands as a testament to both the tragedy that befell this small Texas town and the resilience of those who refused to let evil have the final word.

Online Appendix

Visit my website for additional photos and videos pertaining to the cases in this book:

http://TrueCrimeCaseHistories.com/vol17/

More books by Jason Neal

Looking for more?? I am constantly adding new volumes of True Crime Case Histories. The series **can be read in any order,** and all books are available in paperback, hardcover, and audiobook.

Check out the complete series at:

https://amazon.com/author/jason-neal

All Jason Neal books are also available in **AudioBook format at Audible.com.** Enjoy a **Free Audiobook** when you signup for a 30-Day trial using this link:

https://geni.us/AudibleTrueCrime

TRUE CRIME
BRITISH KILLERS
6 Disturbing True Crime Stories
JASON NEAL

THANK YOU!

Thank you for reading this Volume of True Crime Case Histories. I truly hope you enjoyed it. If you did, I would be sincerely grateful if you would take a few minutes to write a review for me on Amazon using the link below.

https://geni.us/TrueCrime17

I'd also like to encourage you to sign up for my email list for updates, discounts, and freebies on future books! I promise I'll make it worth your while with future freebies.

http://truecrimecasehistories.com

And please take a moment and follow me on Amazon.

http://amazon.com/author/jason-neal/

Thanks so much,

Jason Neal

ABOUT THE AUTHOR

Jason Neal is a Best-Selling American True Crime Author living in Hawaii with his Turkish-British wife. Jason started his writing career in the late eighties as a music industry publisher and wrote his first true crime collection in 2019.

As a boy growing up in the eighties just south of Seattle, Jason became interested in true crime stories after hearing the news of the Green River Killer so close to his home. Over the subsequent years, he would read everything he could get his hands on about true crime and serial killers.

As he approached 50, Jason began to assemble stories of the crimes that have fascinated him most throughout his life. He's especially obsessed by cases solved by sheer luck, amazing police work, and groundbreaking technology like early DNA cases and, more recently, reverse genealogy.

Printed in Great Britain
by Amazon

62894137R00127